CLIENTELLIGENCE

CLIENTELLIGENCE

How Superior Client Relationships
Fuel Growth and Profits

17 Secrets for
Superior Results

Michael B. Rynowecer

THE BTI PRESS

ISBNs: 978-0-9964134-3-5 (hardcover); 978-0-9964134-6-6 (softcover); 978-0-9964134-4-2 (ePub); 978-0-9964134-5-9 (Kindle)
Library of Congress Catalog Number: 2015941707

Printed in the United States of America
First Printing: 2015

19 18 17 16 15   5 4 3 2 1

Cover design by Jennifer Marcus Colligan
Book design by Ryan Scheife / Mayfly Design
and typeset in the Whitman and Lato typefaces

Published by The BTI Press
396 Washington Street, Suite 314
Wellesley, MA 02481
www.thebtipress.com

To be fully and completely seen, undisguised
– NANCY.

Thank you Jennifer Petrone Dezso
for the vision of seeing what is and isn't there.

To all my clients and the decision-makers
who add new thinking to these ideas.

Contents

CLIENTELLIGENCE

Preface

BEHIND EVERY GREAT RAINMAKER, MOVER AND SHAKER AND leader are great relationships. In fact, replace great with superior. People who make things happen make superior relationships first. Relationships are the power source, if not the very soul, of doing good business—the kind of business where clients smile and believe your value simply dwarfs your fee.

People who sell don't develop nearly as much business as people who develop relationships. New business flows to those individuals and companies who can move beyond a transaction to a relationship. People, especially executives, don't want to work with the person with the best sales skills. People want to work with people who are emotionally invested in helping them and will pay significant premiums for this rare commodity.

I wrote this book to define how the people who part with the money—the clients—define and think about superior relationships.

Powerful Insight into the 17 Activities Driving Superior Client Relationships

A long series of in-depth one-on-one interviews with C-level executives revealed 17 specific and unique activities driving superior client relationships. Of these 17 driving factors:

Clients see 4 activities as scarce, delivering the absolute most value and driving hiring decisions on a continuing basis.

You can draw on these primary activities to reap substantially more business from existing clients, in good times or bad. These 4 decisive activities are:

1. Commitment to Help
2. Client Focus
3. Understanding the Client's Business
4. Providing Value for the Dollar

Clients see another 6 of these activities as the "price of admission."

These are the minimum requirements clients set for entering into a relationship. Clients are convinced these activities are widely available from a wide group of competitors. While important, these activities fail to engender enthusiasm or generate more work. Yet this is where most people, companies, and firms focus their client-facing resources.

My hope is you will use these 17 activities to develop more and better relationships—superior relationships—so you don't have to sell, don't have to be moving from client to client, and get access to the best and most challenging work. Your superior relationships will deliver a steady stream of the best work—and yes, superior growth will flow.

Me: "How do you decide who to pick—who to believe—when you need someone to help you with your top issues? How do you know whom to trust?"

EVP Global Energy Company: "I can spot the person who really wants to help me solve my problem; they're invested like no one else. I'll go with them every time."

This short Q&A launched my journey into understanding how and why top executives pick the service providers they do.

In 1989, I founded The BTI Consulting Group and designed a survey to fully understand clients' relationships with their professional services advisors. I set out to define:

- Clients' expectations of their professional services firms
- Why a C-level executive ultimately selects one advisor over another
- How professional services firms leave an imprint on the market

The ultimate goal was to help professional services firms drive:

- More business
- Better client retention
- Improved profitability

Since its inception back in 1989, BTI's survey has grown into the largest known continuous survey defining C-level executive expectations of professional services firms.

At the onset, I expected to hear about client service—it's a vital driver behind nearly every success story in business. But I was looking to dig a little deeper. Much was being made of client service, but very little was being understood. What is the client service secret formula? All clients expect service, but what is it—exactly—they want?

In essence, can client service be quantified?

14,000 in-depth telephone interviews later (back when there were no online survey tools), I had the recipe for how C-level executives define client service.

But before I share the ingredients, why should you care? Let's talk about carbon.

Carbon—the Key to the Best Client Relationships

Carbon is the fundamental element found in both diamonds and charcoal. In the diamond, carbon is highly organized to form a brilliant, long-lasting, valuable commodity. In charcoal, the carbon is arranged in a more random formation, rendering it weak and short-lived; it wears away until it is unusable. Charcoal has its place in the world, but it's not nearly as treasured and revered as its cousin, the diamond.

Now replace "carbon" with "client service."

The more organized your client service activities, the more brilliant, valuable, and enduring your client relationships will be.

My research has isolated 17 activities—key ingredients—essential to delivering superior levels of client service. When you use these activities in a highly organized manner, you can make diamonds of each and every one of your client relationships.

Introduction
Only Clients Can Define Client Service

MY FIRST INTERVIEW WITH THE GLOBAL ENERGY EVP WAS THE basis for a conversation I've now had with more than 14,000 C-level executives.

In its first iteration, the study I conducted allowed for a great deal of latitude from respondents. I was looking to understand what variables C-level executives consider when hiring and assessing their relationships with professional services firms. Within 2 years, I noticed a distinct trend. There was a group of activities identified continuously by executives. But I didn't want to jump to conclusions just yet—I am a researcher after all. Before I was willing to declare a specific activity a true driver of success (more business and better relationships), I had to do more digging.

In order to make this research truly valuable, I needed to go well past a qualitative assessment of client service. It was time to crunch numbers:

- I started by separating out the responses where C-level executives recommend their primary provider in an unprompted manner—meaning the executive would recommend a provider with no prompting of any sort—like a write-in ballot.

  This approach enabled me to start with the relationships where the clients had made an emotional investment (something I would later learn is not only

1

one part of the secret sauce of getting new business at great rates, but the absolute best relationships as well.)

- Once I had identified the invested clients, I looked for spending patterns. Did the professional services firms earning these recommendations actually get more business? In fact, the firms earning unprompted recommendations grew faster than others, as long as they kept earning the unprompted recommendations.

- Many of the recommended professional services firms would see their relationships last longer while others (the firms not recommended) would be replaced. These two observations suggest unprompted recommendations drive both growth and client retention.

The numbers supported the hypothesis:

The professional services firms with the best relationships enjoyed:

- 33% higher client retention
- 8% to 19.5% hourly rate premiums
- 35.9% higher growth rates compared to competitors

I was thrilled. Superior relationships both deliver and drive substantial new business while blocking competitor growth. So, which of all the activities I heard about were really the drivers behind the superior relationships?

Once the second layer of analysis was complete, 17 activities jumped to the top of the list. These activities were the basis for the factors driving new business and the best relationships; the 17 activities provided professional services firms with Clientelligence®.

These activities help professional services firms understand how to transform client interactions into new business and superior relationships. After all, it's not about working harder—it's about working smarter. With the 17 activities in hand, I went out and did what all good analysts do...more research.

The next wave of my research was more pointed. Each C-level executive was asked the obvious question: "How important is each activity to you when you are hiring and evaluating a professional services provider?" I was now able to rank each activity, with the goal of targeting the activities most closely linked to new business.

But the results were slightly underwhelming.

At the top of the list were Domain Skills (meaning the technical skills required to do the job at hand). This flew in the face of every interview I had conducted to date. Based on the conversations I had with hundreds of C-level executives, the top attribute should have been a less tangible attribute directly related to client service—client focus or commitment to help. Yes, being able to do the job was of critical importance, but it didn't drive the best relationships. The data was letting me down.

A dinner conversation with a General Counsel of a Fortune 50 company illuminated the missing piece.

I was discussing the results of my research with this General Counsel when he politely said, "Michael, the data is correct...in a way. I won't hire a law firm unless they have the skills I need. But let's face it, there are hundreds of law firms with the skills I need. The skills are the building blocks. I want to know what the firm is going to build and how committed they are to building it."

The light bulb, metaphorically, came on.

The next day, I revamped my interview guide to include the following question: "How easy is it for you to find a professional services firm able to deliver superior levels of each activity?"

The new question blew the doors open. The activities, when assessed on these 2 dimensions, fell into distinct groups and painted a clear picture of client relationships.

The Clientelligence Matrix

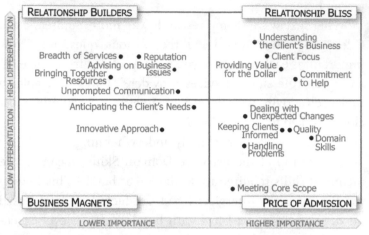

Despite the inherent intuitiveness of this chart, let me take a quick moment to explain what you're seeing.

How The Clientelligence Matrix Works

The horizontal axis of The Clientelligence Matrix represents the relative importance of each activity. Activities on the right side of the chart are more important to C-level executives than activities on the left side.

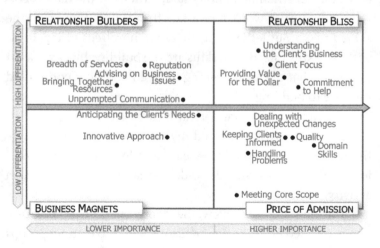

How The Clientelligence Matrix Works

The vertical axis of The Clientelligence Matrix represents the strength of each activity's ability to differentiate a professional services firm. Activities on the top half of the chart are harder for C-level executives to find in a professional services firm—making them strong differentiators.

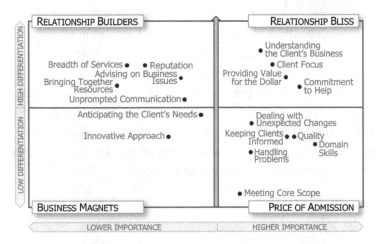

The Quadrants: The 100-foot View

Each quadrant in this chart exhibits distinct characteristics and plays an important role in developing and maintaining superior relationships with C-level executives.

Quadrant I: Relationship Bliss

4 activities are the most important to C-level executives and provide high levels of differentiation for you and your firm. In short, these are the central ingredients critical to superior client service and long-lasting client relationships.

These activities are scarce in the market and drive hiring decisions on a continuing basis. Professional services firms can draw on these primary activities to reap substantially more business from existing clients and draw in new clients—in good times or bad.

1. Commitment to Help
2. Client Focus
3. Understanding the Client's Business
4. Providing Value for the Dollar

Quadrant II: Price of Admission

C-level executives see 6 activities as the minimum requirements for entering into a relationship with a professional services firm.

The activities in the lower-right quadrant are of the highest importance, but they are also widely available in the market. Meaning: you must demonstrate these activities in order to win work, but they do not differentiate you enough to be the sole decision criteria used in hiring.

5. Domain Skills
6. Quality
7. Meeting Core Scope
8. Keeping the Client Informed
9. Dealing with Unexpected Changes
10. Handling Problems

Quadrant III: Relationship Builders

5 activities stand out as providing high differentiation for the firms able to deliver them.

Since these activities are of lower importance to C-level executives, on their own they are simply "nice to have;" they won't solidify a relationship over the long term.

11. Breadth of Services
12. Advising on Business Issues
13. Reputation

14. Unprompted Communication
15. Bringing Together Resources

Quadrant IV: Business Magnets

Few activities capture the eyes of leading C-level executives quicker than the activities in the lower-left quadrant.

These activities are an anomaly of sorts, pushing them into the lower-left quadrant. Initially, these activities would seem to be less important and less differentiating for professional services firms. However, when I looked at the research in segments, what I found was the least price-sensitive clients with the most complex needs seek out these 2 activities. These are the types of clients most professional services firms are most interesting in courting.

16. Anticipating the Client's Needs
17. Innovative Approach

Pulling It Together: The Complete Guide to the 17 Activities

While certain activities on their own will benefit your client relationships, the best results and long-term success demand you deliver the optimal blend of each of the 17 activities. Much like cooking, too much of one ingredient or not enough of another can throw the whole recipe off—regardless of whether or not you use the finest ingredients in the world. The taste depends on how everything comes together in the completed dish.

Let's dive into the recipe for delivering superior client service to drive the absolute best relationships with C-level executives.

> And see the Pull It Together charts, starting in Chapter 5, for tips on communication techniques proven to demonstrate your value, commitment, client focus, and understanding of the client's business.

Relationship Bliss

The Most Strategic—
and Financially Rewarding—Activities

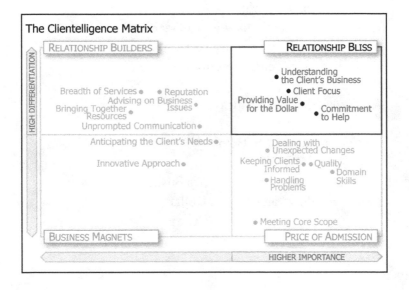

The Clientelligence Matrix

RELATIONSHIP BUILDERS

RELATIONSHIP BLISS

HIGH DIFFERENTIATION

- Breadth of Services
- Reputation
- Advising on Business Issues
- Bringing Together Resources
- Unprompted Communication

- Understanding the Client's Business
- Client Focus
- Providing Value for the Dollar
- Commitment to Help

- Anticipating the Client's Needs
- Innovative Approach

- Dealing with Unexpected Changes
- Keeping Clients Informed
- Quality
- Domain Skills
- Handling Problems

- Meeting Core Scope

BUSINESS MAGNETS

PRICE OF ADMISSION

HIGHER IMPORTANCE

Relationship Bliss:
Higher Importance / Higher Differentiation

The 4 activities in this quadrant are the most important to C-level executives and will most differentiate your firm from competitors. The ability to excel in these 4 activities will not only build stronger client relationships, but more profitable ones as well.

My 30 years of research have proven the professional services firms able to deliver best-in-class levels (a quantitative measurement you can read more about in the Appendix) in these 4 activities will outpace competitors not performing at peak levels in terms of:

- 30% higher profits
- 7% rate premiums across all staffing levels
- Double the fees from a single client
- 35% higher client retention

The 4 powerhouse activities driving Relationship Bliss are:

1. Commitment to Help
2. Client Focus
3. Understanding the Client's Business
4. Providing Value for the Dollar

CHAPTER 1

Commitment to Help
Say, "I Do" to Your Clients

> **Question:** *In a bacon and egg breakfast, what's the difference between the chicken and the pig?*
> **Answer:** *The chicken is involved, but the pig is committed.*
>
> Most of the time, being called a pig is not a compliment. But if clients think you are a pig, it is the ultimate seal of approval.

The caller ID flashed on the ringing phone and Jonathan, the Chief Legal Officer of a Fortune 100 company, immediately tensed. The display showed 10:06 AM and Jonathan knew the number was his law school buddy, Lori, now working at the Securities and Exchange Commission. Jonathan picked up the receiver and said a friendly hello.

Lori shared pleasantries, but the tone quickly changed. Lori informed Jonathan that the agency, after months of study, was preparing to launch a formal investigation into the company's accounting practices. Immediately, Jonathan envisioned the disclosures, the inevitable drop in the stock price of his company, the exodus of customers, and the harsh scrutiny of the company's shareholders. His face went white thinking of the bill attached to managing the investigation and follow-up rulings.

Jonathan wanted to move quickly and decisively. Once he hung up with Lori, he immediately called his go-to legal advisor, Bart. Bart was a litigator at one of the 20 largest law firms in the world. The 2 had worked together for more than 15 years and there was no voice Jonathan wanted to hear more. When Bart picked up the phone, Jonathan shared the news.

Bart, understanding the gravity of the situation, shared his sympathies and quickly reminded Jonathan, "SEC and accounting investigations aren't in my wheelhouse. However, I don't want you to worry. Last year, we brought on a new partner who has tremendous experience in these types of matters." Bart went on, "This guy is based out of our West Coast office, so he's a few hours behind us. I'll give his assistant a ring and have an appointment scheduled for the 3 of us as quickly as possible." Before they hung up, Bart confided, "Now, please understand. This partner's going rate starts at $1,100 an hour—I just want you to be prepared for a little sticker shock."

The 2 hung up. Jonathan stared at the phone, afraid it would ring again. He knew his CEO would be calling any minute demanding an action plan and Jonathan had nothing. He reached for the phone and dialed Deborah, another attorney he had worked with recently on a handful of major matters. Jonathan hoped Deborah would have some quick advice for him.

Once patched through to Deborah, Jonathan begain retelling the details of the SEC decision. Deborah quietly listened and afterwards asked if she could put Jonathan on hold for a few minutes. Jonathan placed the call on speaker, muted the line, and responded to a handful of emails while he waited. 11 minutes later, Deborah returned to the line and introduced Jonathan to Gary and Susan—2 experienced SEC attorneys ready to start brainstorming next steps with Jonathan.

Post Script: Later in the afternoon, Bart's assistant called back to schedule a meeting between Jonathan, Bart, and their West Coast SEC attorney. Jonathan was on his second conference call with Deborah and her partners and didn't return the call.

Jonathan ultimately spent more than $33 million dollars with Deborah's firm.

This a true story and one I've heard many times—admittedly on a smaller scale than in the tale of Jonathan and Bart.

Poor Bart. He's a pig in hiding. His heart was in the right place, but he sent out a bevy of unintended messages suggesting he was a chicken.

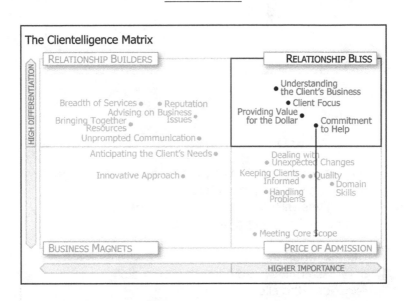

Commitment to help is the single most important factor to C-level executives when they evaluate and hire professional services firms.

In the Clientelligence Matrix above, you see commitment to help is more important (further to the right) than everything but domain skills, and domain skills—whether or not you can even do the work—as we discuss in Chapter 5, have no influence on the relationship unless these skills are lacking.

Your commitment to help clients will make—or break—the most meaningful client relationships.

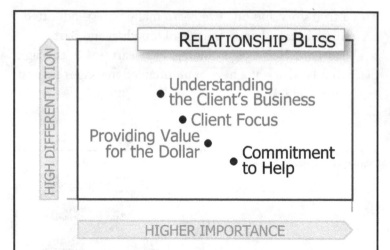

Navigating the Quadrants

Every client brings their own definition of commitment to help. It is a subjective assessment C-level executives will make to determine how invested you are in the client relationship.

Clients report the best relationships with professional services firms whose commitment matches—or exceeds—the client's.

While every client will define commitment in a slightly different way, they will all ask themselves the same question in order to test your investment:

"Are you here to bill hours *or* are you here to truly help me solve my problem/reach my goal?"

This is a black or white question—all or nothing. You are either the most committed, or you aren't. Your clients will look at the verbal and non-verbal cues you send out. Every action, inaction, response, and behavior will be analyzed and, whether intentional or not, will speak volumes about your commitment.

Do your clients see you as a pig or a chicken?

In order to prove your pig-ness, a professional must go beyond the boundaries of a typical commercial relationship. Call it engagement, investment, or commitment—clients want you to match (or exceed) their own levels of:

- Urgency
- Energy
- Perceived investment of time, money, and psychic energy

While Deborah, in the above anecdote, addressed Jonathan's most pressing need in an urgent manner, Bart was talking about rates and overlooked the client's need for immediate action. Bart was being helpful, not committed.

Clientelligence Master Class:

Delivering Best-in-Class Performances on the Most Strategic Activities

---

How committed are you?

Superhero Pigs

The most committed professionals are always looking for opportunities to help. These superheroes are easy to spot (the pig wearing a cape is hard to miss) because they:

- Have constant open communication with clients. Superheroes seem to know everything about their clients—both professionally and personally—from business objectives, new work needs, personal challenges, to the names of their clients' dogs. Superheroes are always gathering information and using it to anticipate client needs and avoid lurking issues.

- (Seemingly) never sleep. Superheroes don't stop until the client's goal has been met—no matter how difficult or time constrained the project may be. There is little room for compromise in urgent situations.

- Take bullets for their clients. Egos take a back seat when you are proving your commitment to clients. When things go wrong, superheroes quickly step up and take accountability (and offer solutions to correct the situation). Not only does this approach save time, it lets the client save face with top management. Superheroes are true allies.

- Go the extra mile—or 10. Superheroes pull off seemingly amazing feats to help clients succeed. Success goes beyond delivering outcomes. Clients are looking for personal success and superheroes get them there by helping with anything from being published, to teaching positions, to the best table at top restaurants for a special anniversary. Superheroes pull in favors to demonstrate commitment to their clients.

- Are direct—not contrary. Superheroes will tell clients the truth, no matter how unpopular the opinion may be. These advisors take their responsibility as guides seriously. Their experience, knowledge, and understanding drive recommendations. They don't simply recite what they hope the client wants to hear.

Power Mongers

At the core, the power monger's commitment rivals the superhero's. They leap into action, mobilizing resources, ensuring deadlines are met, and guaranteeing the client's goal is met as promised. However, power mongers have trouble demonstrating their commitment to help on a regular basis. When the water gets hot, they perform best, but on a more routine basis they tend to lose focus on true commitment.

Another difference between power mongers and superheroes is their communication style with clients. Whereas superheroes have developed an informal, easy communication style with clients, power mongers—enjoying the heat of the battle—frequently forget to keep clients in the loop. Progress and budget updates happen when deadlines roll around and bills are submitted. The client ends up being the last to know about a change in budget or scope.

Power mongers often turn into superheroes once trained to share their considerable prowess, talent, and thought processes with the client.

Contractors

Do you find yourself boasting, "I gave the client just what they asked for—and the project was on time and on budget!"

Contractors are highly skilled and use their skills to fulfill the scope of work for the task at hand. They bring little emotion to their work—feeling concerned with getting the job done—but not always matching the client's urgency concerning a

(continued on next page)

(continued from previous page)

project. Communication is a tool to keep projects on track—nothing more, nothing less.

Without urgency, contractors find themselves rarely considered for high-value, complex, or risk-oriented work.

High-powered Lemmings (HPLs)

HPLs are your yes-men. They look to clients for direction, advice, and, problematically, for solutions. At the slightest hint of controversy, HPLs will hide behind the client, asking for their thoughts on next steps (but never offering their own ideas).

Resistors

Naysayers, progress blockers, and Debbie Downers. Resistors seem to always find a reason for why something can't be done—instead of figuring out how to get it done. These dangerous professionals see the world fraught with risk, strict rules, and consequences when rules are broken. In fact, their commitment to the rules supersedes their commitment to the client.

However, even resistors have a role. Resistors are often technically savvy and have a keen ability to project the roadblocks ahead, but they offer little in the way of solutions. This makes the resistor an excellent sounding board for superheroes and power mongers—but on a stand-alone basis, they rarely incite commitment.

———

Maintaining superhero status is hard work, but they are the competition you are up against every day. Anything less than *Superhero Pig* is *Chicken the Villain*.

CHAPTER 2

Client Focus

Stop Providing the Best Possible Solution

A FEW YEARS AGO, I CONDUCTED AN INTERESTING STUDY. I spoke to both C-level executives and to their professional services providers to determine how each group defined client focus. The results were astounding.

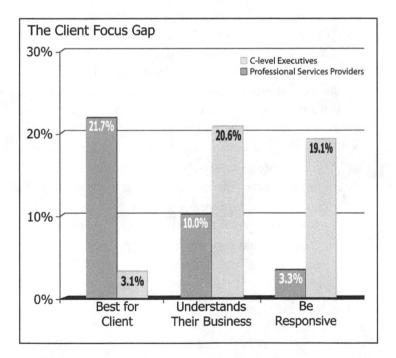

A professional's first instinct is to do the best job possible. Provide undisputable advice—the 24-karat gold solution. C-level executives want you to meet their targeted needs. You can argue both populations are essentially saying, "do what's best," but the distinction is in who gets to decide what's best. We call this misalignment the Client Focus Gap.

The quest for the best solution can make even the most savvy, thoughtful professional tone deaf. They are unable to hear the nuances of the client's goals in their search for the perfect answer. I frequently see professionals get irate in their arguments with clients as they explain the stringent quality and technical standards to which they applied their solution. And while clients can appreciate this, if the solution doesn't meet their targeted needs, it is a failure.

The Client Focus Gap has claimed many victims:

- A group of engineers designed a piping system with a 25-year life span—in a plant with a 10-year non-renewable lease (read the whole story in Chapter 6).
- An ecommerce consultant recommended his middle-market retail client implement a payment platform. Unfortunately it didn't accept the payment method used by 40% of their customers.
- Environmental consultants from a global firm recommended a site clean-up strategy requiring trucks hauling contaminated dirt across the main security gate of a refinery every 20 minutes—for 6 years.
- A marketing agency created an engaging new website for their national consumer products clients, but Google couldn't read any of the text on the page. Overnight, organic searches to the website dropped 40%.

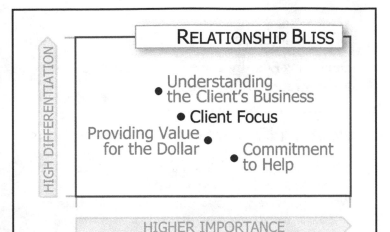

RELATIONSHIP BLISS

HIGH DIFFERENTIATION

• Understanding
  the Client's Business

• Client Focus

Providing Value •
for the Dollar •
        • Commitment
          to Help

HIGHER IMPORTANCE

Navigating the Quadrants

Client focus is the ability to deliver on your client's targeted outcome. Client-targeted outcomes can be—and usually are—vastly different from the academically best outcome.

Client outcomes are driven by business goals, budget constraints, and risk tolerance.

Clientelligence Master Class:

Delivering Best-in-Class Performances on the Most Strategic Activities

---

Close the Client Focus Gap.

The only way to avoid falling into the Client Focus Gap is to completely understand your client's targeted outcome. While many professionals ask clients about their objectives, an astonishing 79% of providers do not actively confirm their clients' goals before beginning work on a project.

The most common, best-intentioned reasons for not confirming client goals are:

- "I know my client like the back of my hand."
- "It's obvious what the client is looking for."
- "My client will think I don't understand or am incompetent if I ask."
- "I don't want to bother my client."
- "Confirming objectives is a waste of time. It's redundant to what we've already talked about."

Why do I stress the importance of confirming client objectives? Simple: objectives change.

How many of your clients have gone through one of the following:

- New strategic or business plans
- Reorganization or layoffs
- Economic uncertainty in the market
- IPO
- Acquisitions, divestitures, or other transactions
- Lower-than-anticipated stock performance, earnings shortfalls

Changes are inevitable and will greatly impact your client's goals and strategic direction.

1. Ask your client about their objectives—before you start work
2. Probe as to how your client defines success
3. Discuss any management mandates and pressure your client faces
4. Actively confirm client goals and objectives, in writing
5. Include your client in your thought process before making major decisions
6. Share—and obtain feedback—on potential solutions with your client as you are performing the work, not afterwards

Once you understand your client's goals, you are ready to provide custom, tailored services to best meet their needs.

CHAPTER 3

Understanding the Client's Business

Do You Get Me? I Mean Really Get Me?

> *"Seek first to understand, then to be understood."*
> —Dr. Stephen R. Covey

Before we had children, my wife and I had everything planned out. Our children would most certainly not be the usual tantrum-throwing toddlers running rampant in the grocery store aisles or the always dirty, disheveled boys telling off-color jokes at inopportune times. Luckily, we kept our lofty dreams to ourselves because 5 years later, I found myself attempting every negotiation tactic I had learned in business school just to get my oldest son to eat a piece of chicken while my younger son was in the kitchen playing in the dog's water bowl.

It's safe to say before we had kids, we just didn't understand.

Now with 20-plus years of experience under our belts, we've managed to raise 2 successful men who make us proud.

The word "understand" is an interesting one. The ancient Greeks used the word "epistamai" to express understanding, which roughly translates to "to be close to." The more modern translation offered by Merriam-Webster defines "understand" as "to be thoroughly familiar with the character and propensities of."

In short, if we are to achieve true understanding—whether in parenting or a client's business—we are required to be close to and thoroughly familiar with the situation and environment in which we find ourselves.

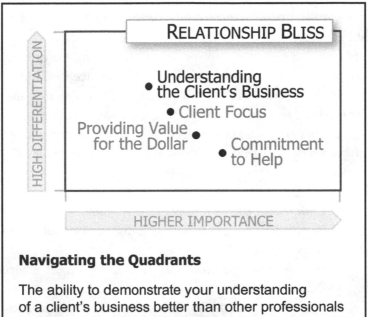

Navigating the Quadrants

The ability to demonstrate your understanding of a client's business better than other professionals is the single most powerful differentiator in the eyes of clients. C-level executives seek out professional services providers able to offer targeted recommendations and guidance in the context of the client's business.

The most valuable and sought-after advice takes into account industry dynamics, business objectives, current events, and competitive pressures.

People Love to Be Understood

The more you understand your clients, the more relevant your work will be for them. Your comprehension of a client's world—the challenges they face, the goals they have, the opportunities there are to drive success—is the glue used to bind the strongest, longest-lasting client relationships.

C-level executives will seek out and pay premium rates for counsel they trust. This is the guidance of advisors who understand the full scope of an issue and all the implications the client needs to consider before making a decision. Professional services providers unable to provide their advice in the context of the client's business will quickly find themselves a one-time vendor instead of a long-standing business partner.

Clients aren't the only ones who benefit from your depth of knowledge on their business. Building a comprehensive understanding of the client's business will position you to:

- Understand what your client really wants
- Be the first to tackle the defining issues your client faces
- Provide more pointed, targeted, and relevant advice than competitors
- Proactively identify business, financial, and political issues (to help your client and build business)
- Anticipate and plan for business risks
- Help your client implement your recommendations

Clientelligence Master Class:

Delivering Best-in-Class Performances on the Most Strategic Activities

The 3 stages of comprehensive business understanding

Building an in-depth, unmatched understanding of a client's business is time-consuming, can fluctuate between tedious and exhilarating, but ultimately opens doors to the most complex, highest-rate work your clients manage. Delivering results in the context of the client's business solidifies your position as the go-to provider of choice.

The payoff is worth the work

Now, clients are not expecting you to bring a detailed operating knowledge of their business. Just because you do work for a major manufacturer doesn't mean you should be able to fix a machine on the assembly line when it breaks down. Clients value core business understanding such as:

- Fundamental business strategies
- Business and product lines
- Risk tolerance
- Business events (acquisitions, divestitures, new top management)
- Core operating principles and organizational relationships (i.e., know how one function potentially impacts another)

There are 3 stages to building a comprehensive understanding of the client's business:

(continued on next page)

(continued from previous page)

Stage 1: Entry-level understanding

In today's world, building your basic understanding of a client's business has never been easier. But mining the client's website, following news feeds, and setting up client-specific alerts through Google are baby steps when developing the level of knowledge needed to outpace competitors.

This information is where all service providers start. It certainly does not provide you with enough information to develop insights other competitors—or even the clients themselves—would miss.

Stage 2: Extreme understanding

Few service providers ever enter Stage 2 when building their understanding of a client's business. Coupling your experience and advice with targeted client insight begins to differentiate you in the eyes of clients. The following tools—all readily available—will provide you with a wealth of client insight and information:

- Comprehensive alerts and news tracking—go beyond tracking only the client organization's name and set up your newsfeeds to include:
  > Individual client brand, trade, and subsidiary names
  > Top executives, by name
  > Competitor organizations
    » The same information you're tracking on clients (brands, subsidiaries, executives, etc.)
  > Activity at major government agencies and ruling bodies (US Patent and Trademark Office, SEC, etc.)
  > Stock prices for publicly held organizations
  > Job listings at the company
    » If your client is suddenly hiring an EVP of Global Transactions, it's a strong indicator of some M&A activity on the horizon

- Listen to earnings calls for publicly held clients (and their major competitors)
  - > This is one of the most underutilized information sources available. During these calls, companies often announce new initiatives, strategy changes, and market trends—information professional services firms can use for targeted business development and client-focused recommendations
- Read everything you can including:
  - > 10K filings (don't skip over the Management Discussion and Analysis section)
  - > Financial statements—including the footnotes
  - > Client business and strategic plans (most clients are happy to share these with their professional services providers)
- Read even more
  - > Ask your client to recommend the best books for you to read in order to better understand their business, then read them
  - > Subscribe to local business journals in areas where your client has major facilities
  - > Scan industry reports and even stock analyst opinions on the client organization
- Get information directly from the source
  - > Systematically meet with clients—outside the current scope of work—to discuss business goals, issues, and forward-looking plans
  - > Take a facility tour
  - > Leverage social media for breaking news; follow the client on Twitter, LinkedIn, and Facebook

As busy professionals, this list is overwhelming—if not impossible—for one person to handle. Leverage the junior professionals at your organization to bring this information together in a systematic, digestible manner. Not only does

(continued on next page)

(continued from previous page)

this leverage your time, you are also teaching your staff the importance of understanding the client's business.

Stage 3: Integrated understanding

It's time to share everything you've learned with the client. Integrated understanding—the most powerful understanding—brings your insight and understanding together with the client's to achieve the most relevant, highest quality results possible. This does not mean you need to provide a presentation to a client on their business. Rather, integrate your understanding into everything you do for the client such as:

- Include a conversation around the business implications of all guidance and advice you offer
- Proactively help clients spot, track, and mitigate potential issues in current work and in other areas of the organization or market
- Take unequivocal stands on your recommendations by discussing the strategic thought process and impacts of your recommendations throughout the organization and in the market
- Offer strategies to streamline business processes, control costs, and better prepare internal resources

Every deliverable, email, phone call, and interaction you have with a client is your opportunity to demonstrate your knowledge of their business. Clients are only interested in the outcomes. Discussing your analysis, advice, and recommendations in the context of the client's business showcases your focus on helping them reach their desired endpoint.

CHAPTER 4

Providing Value for the Dollar

You Win on Value. You Lose on Price.

Jonah felt a sense of panic. As the Chief Safety Officer of Buy Our Products (BOP) Inc., Jonah had just learned an OSHA inspector had found a number of violations at their main manufacturing facility. Out of 273 production machines, BOP Inc. was cited for 63 instances of missing safety devices on their manufacturing equipment.

Jonah conducted his own internal investigation and determined the safety devices weren't missing, but instead had been modified. After speaking with employees on the floor, he discovered the employees removed part of the safety device to boost productivity (and consequently, their pay). Despite BOP Inc.'s clear policy and intended system for preventing this work-around, employees would remove the devices anyway.

Jonah knew fixing the devices was simple. Keeping the incident from becoming a brand-destroying event was the bigger challenge. In recent years, BOP Inc. had become extraordinarily sensitive to corporate citizenship, not to mention the potential $1 million fine would also raise eyebrows with management and the press.

Jonah called Darren, a renowned consultant for these matters. Darren immediately understood the implications and the issues and jumped head-first into his mission. First, he found precedent to have this infraction treated as a single incident instead of 63. Darren also discovered settled cases where a partial device was acceptable for safety purposes, indicating there may not have been a violation at all.

Darren penned a deal with the regulatory agency. Rather than pay the substantial $1 million fine, BOP, Inc. would pay a $160,000 fee to cover the cost of investigation and the company would have to agree to mandatory training and proof of compliance with the safety regulation. All of this was achieved with little fanfare and there was no need for BOP Inc. to disclose any of the issues or subsequent proceedings. Darren reported this outcome to a quite pleased Jonah.

4 months later, Jonah received Darren's invoice for a total fee of $134,611.20.

Jonah studied the 6-page bill. The invoice listed hundreds of time entries detailing Darren's time in 15-minute increments. Virtually all the time entries were categorized as "Meeting/Conference." Jonah called Darren to ask why the invoice was so high relative to the fee paid to the agency, "Your fee is only $30,000 less than what we paid the inspectors. This feels a little out of proportion, particularly since you spent most of your time in meetings."

Darren was dumbfounded. After a brief pause, he explained the nuances of how he had spent his time. Darren reminded Jonah of the long hours he and his compliance specialist had spent negotiating with OSHA and the extra finesse needed when dealing with the agency became difficult.

Despite the outcome delivered, Darren's value was destroyed.

Your Client's Perception Is Your Client's Reality

What do you see in the picture above?

It's a famous perceptual illusion. Some of you will immediately see an older woman, while others will first see a younger woman. No matter which figure you initially see, with a little prompting, your eyes can quickly be guided to see the other (the chin of the younger woman whose face is turned away is the nose of the older woman's side profile).

This is how value works with your clients.

Clients will interpret your value according to what they perceive: usually an incomplete, one-sided picture. Clients need your guidance to accurately see the whole picture, including the less obvious and sometimes hidden ways in which you delivered value to the client.

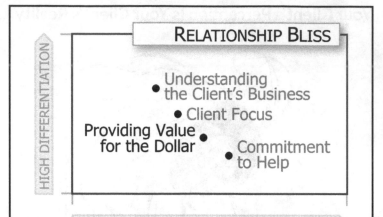

RELATIONSHIP BLISS

HIGH DIFFERENTIATION

- Understanding
  the Client's Business
  - Client Focus

Providing Value
  for the Dollar
  - Commitment
    to Help

HIGHER IMPORTANCE

Navigating the Quadrants

Delivering value is dependent on being able to articulate exactly what it is you provided for your clients—no matter how obvious you think your actions are.

Communicating value requires talking to clients in terms they understand and consider important: money saved, increased revenue streams, faster time to market, risks avoided, and better outcomes than anticipated.

We Are the Enemy

You are your own worst enemy when it comes to delivering superior value—and not because you don't deliver it. The overwhelming majority of professionals tend to keep the substantial value they deliver a deep, dark secret.

What clients view as valuable, we consider part of the job. We neglect to share the intense problem-solving and challenging roadblocks we overcame in order to meet the client's objectives. We deliver what the client expected, all while making the most difficult of tasks look easy.

The final insult comes when our client receives an invoice reflecting the hours and hours of hard work we endured. Hours, which due to circumstances out of our control, may not have been included in the original budget. Rather than applauding you for your ingenious solution or ability to avoid a much larger issue, all the client sees is: you blew past the budget.

In order to understand how we can better articulate our value to clients, we first need to understand how clients assess value. Unfortunately, it's more new math than true math. Fully 85% of C-level executives look at the insights and outcomes from a project and assign their own subjective value. Their formula (at its most basic) reads:

Value = Perception of Services Delivered – Expectations of Services Delivered

[Translation for the non-math inclined: Value is achieved when a provider delivers more than what is expected.]

To be perceived as a value builder, you must work this formula to your advantage. Like the optical illusion at the start of this chapter, you must guide and shape your client's perception of the value you brought to their project. When we successfully add value to our client relationships, it changes the client's perception of us from a simple vendor to a trusted counselor.

Darren, in the story above, is one of a large group of professionals who presume the value they bring to their clients is obvious for all to see. Let me be the first to tell you, **what is obvious to you is oblivion to your client**. The client (Jonah) had lost sight of the savings Darren afforded BOP Inc. against a proposed $1 million fine. In the 4 months from the project resolution to the receipt of the bill, Jonah had also forgotten the potential reputational damages Darren had avoided.

Let's be clear here: Darren also did not effectively articulate the value he was providing to BOP Inc. and Jonah. When a client sees a bill 4 months later without a note or client-friendly explanation, it's hard for them to remember the original value you delivered.

Unlike you, clients are not singularly focused on the one project we are handling for them. Additionally, you are not the only professional services provider working with your client. The fact is the typical client—regardless of industry or profession—works with 4 to 11 of your direct competitors every day. 4 to 11 other firms are stealing your client's attention, making noise, or pitching their own value to your client.

Darren is not alone in his failure to clearly articulate the value he delivered to his client. It is the rare professional who is able to help their client understand the true—and full—value of the services delivered. My research reveals 6 drivers behind professionals' reluctance to talk about value with their clients:

1. Fear of stating the obvious
2. Impressions of bothering the client
3. Not wanting to appear self-serving
4. Lack of time
5. Unsure they truly delivered value
6. Inability to accurately measure the value provided

Before I discuss how to combat the misconceptions above, let me talk about the one surprising factor we haven't yet mentioned in this chapter: rates.

Professional services firms providing value do not slash rates or undercut the competition. Continually lowering rates and offering large discounts has actually been shown to erode a client's perception of your value. Rather, the most successful professional services providers communicate the value they deliver in a manner rendering rate discussions a benign afterthought. In short, these providers show clients how the value they delivered far exceeded the price the client paid.

Clientelligence Master Class:

Delivering Best-in-Class Performances on the Most Strategic Activities

---

Be a value builder (not a value destroyer).

Delivering value is one of the most powerful ways to differentiate your firm in the eyes of your clients. When C-level executives feel they receive more than what they paid for, they become the most loyal clients who are willing to pay premium rates.

Professionals who are masters in the art of articulating value are able to:

- Make clients feel smarter for having hired the right advisor
- Teach clients how to articulate their own value to top management—helping the client and the advisor be better positioned with key decision makers
- Use scope changes and unexpected issues to deliver more value to clients

Make clients feel smarter for having hired the right advisor

Value builders share every major breakthrough, problem solved, and obstacle overcome with their clients. C-level executives understand, recognize, and appreciate the work required to overcome obstacles. Rather than see it as over-communication, clients thank their advisors for timely updates and the resolution of potentially major issues.

Teach clients how to articulate their own value to top management

The first rule in articulating your own value to C-level executives is to speak in terms the client understands and considers important. Most organizations include the metrics for success in their business and strategic planning initiatives. Discuss (or even better, read) the plans with your client to understand the terminology they use and the factors they consider most important. While each client is different, there are some universal benefits clients find valuable. The more you talk about how you delivered these "extras," the more valuable you are perceived to be. These extras include:

- Time saved
  - > Expedited deliverables, filings, deals, processes, settlements
  - > Help clients get to market faster
- Costs avoided
  - > Cut costs without cutting prices
  - > Eliminate need for hardware
  - > Bundle services
  - > Significantly reduce licensing or processing fees
- Risks mitigated
  - > Anticipate regulatory hurdles
  - > Improve protection of key assets
- Dramatically better outcomes than expected

Note: nowhere in the above list does it mention providing exemplary skills or showcasing your extensive expertise. Those attributes got you hired. Doing what you were hired to do is not value added to clients.

When you start articulating your value in the above terms, you're now speaking the client's language. When you speak the client's language, they have the tools to report to their top management and key stakeholders in terms easily understood—making everyone look smart.

(continued on next page)

(continued from previous page)

Use scope changes and unexpected issues to deliver more value to clients

More than 80% of professional services projects—design, litigation, transactions, web development, software development, training, environmental remediation, construction, and everything else you can imagine—include changes in scope (see Chapter 7 for a more detailed discussion).

Most professionals presume clients know when the scope has changed and understand the impact on deliverables, timelines, and budgets. The reality is scope typically changes in small increments—a small change here, a minor revision there—but over time, scope changes add up to a large deviance from the original project parameters.

Value builders are communication masters. Before any value is destroyed, they ensure clients are aware of the impact of each change—in a client-friendly, value-added manner.

- Confirm scope changes with clients in real-time
- Outline the full implications of these changes on the client's original goals before discussing your fees
  - > This demonstrates your client-focused commitment to the overriding objectives
- After discussing the implications you can discuss the equally important impact on budget, resources, timing, etc.
- Proactively share your recommendations for handling any changes in order to keep the original parameters as intact as possible

WRAP-UP

Quadrant I
Relationship Bliss

So, why didn't I just save everyone some time and only write a book about these 4 activities if they are the ones most closely tied to growth?

You may remember at the very beginning of the book, I talked about how each of the 17 activities in this book were the ones C-level executives rely on to drive the best relationships. While the 4 activities in the Relationship Bliss quadrant have the strongest statistical correlation to financial benefit, every activity has a crucial role in the development, maintenance, and ultimate growth of client relationships. Overlook the

The Clientelligence Matrix

RELATIONSHIP BUILDERS — RELATIONSHIP BLISS

HIGH DIFFERENTIATION

Breadth of Services • • Reputation
Advising on Business
Bringing Together • Issues •
Resources •
Unprompted Communication •

• Understanding
the Client's Business
• Client Focus
Providing Value •
for the Dollar • Commitment
to Help

Anticipating the Client's Needs •

Innovative Approach •

Dealing with
• Unexpected Changes
Keeping Clients • • Quality
Informed • Domain
• Handling Skills
Problems

• Meeting Core Scope

BUSINESS MAGNETS — PRICE OF ADMISSION

HIGHER IMPORTANCE

power of Relationship Builders and opportunities for organic growth with your existing clients may be missed. Without the Price of Admission activities, clients won't even consider hiring you. Failure to demonstrate your ability in the Business Magnets could cost you some of the highest-spending clients.

Every activity will bring you one step closer to having superior relationships with your clients. You get there quicker—and the payoff is higher—when you focus on the Relationship Bliss activities. These activities can and do make you better at the other 13 activities. However, you will benefit more by making links between the activities to drive even better performance faster.

QUADRANT II

The Price of Admission

6 Activities Required to Be Considered for Work

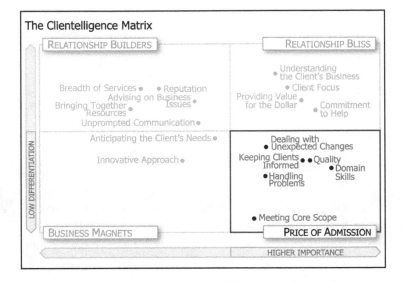

The Clientelligence Matrix

RELATIONSHIP BUILDERS — RELATIONSHIP BLISS

Understanding
the Client's Business
Client Focus
Breadth of Services • • Reputation
Advising on Business
Bringing Together • Issues
Resources
Unprompted Communication •

Providing Value
for the Dollar • Commitment
to Help

Anticipating the Client's Needs •

Dealing with
Unexpected Changes
Keeping Clients • • Quality
Informed • Domain
• Handling Skills
Problems

Innovative Approach •

• Meeting Core Scope

BUSINESS MAGNETS — PRICE OF ADMISSION

LOW DIFFERENTIATION

HIGHER IMPORTANCE

The Price of Admission:
Higher Importance / Lower Differentiation

If you can't bring the basics, a client won't even entertain the notion of entering into a relationship with you. Never mind give you more business.

The bottom-right quadrant is home to the activities C-level executives find of utmost importance. These are core requirements without which a C-level executive will not even consider you or your firm to handle their work. However, these activities are also abundantly available in the marketplace. In short, these activities will not help you stand apart from the competition.

Clients expect you to come armed with the following:

5. Domain Skills
6. Quality
7. Meeting Core Scope
8. Keeping the Client Informed
9. Dealing with Unexpected Changes
10. Handling Problems

Most professional services firms are deeply focused on these 6 activities. After all, without them you will not win work. However, relationships built around just these 6 activities are unstable. These activities are essentially available from every service provider—think of them as the commodities of client service. And like any commodity, without qualitative differentiation, the market will buy on price alone.

This is not how we want to do business.

I could tell you to deliver, but don't overly focus on, these 6 price-of-admission activities. Since they're not high differentiators, you could do the bare minimum and spend your time on the higher impact activities in the Clientelligence Matrix. But even within these commodity-service attributes there are ways to leverage how you deliver these activities to differentiate your firm and move you higher up the list of potential firms a C-level executive is considering hiring.

Higher on the list = more likely to be hired. And winning the work is the first step to building a long-lasting, profitable relationship with clients.

CHAPTER 5

Domain Skills
Telling Clients You Are Potty Trained

SOMEWHERE BETWEEN 18 MONTHS AND 3-YEARS OF AGE, YOU began potty training. Initially you were filled with excitement and fear, but you were given encouragement, guidance, and rewards. Even despite some embarrassment and reprimands, you continued to work hard.

The more you practiced, the better you got. Soon you were proudly touting your potty skills—announcing to everyone within earshot when you needed "to go" and parading your way to the restroom.

After a few near (and actual) misses, you took control of your skills. Within a short timeframe, you became accustomed to your newfound abilities. And while they were still important, you didn't make an announcement every time you needed a potty break. Your skills became second nature and were no longer something requiring much thought.

You have since learned to visit the restroom before a long trip. You quietly slip in and out of marathon meetings for bio breaks. In short, you stopped emphasizing your potty skills because...well...everyone has them.

Domain skills—your technical capabilities—are the potty training of your professional life.

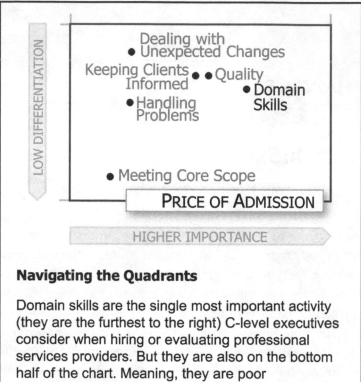

LOW DIFFERENTIATION

Dealing with
● Unexpected Changes
Keeping Clients ● ● Quality
Informed   ● **Domain**
● Handling   **Skills**
Problems

● Meeting Core Scope

PRICE OF ADMISSION

HIGHER IMPORTANCE

Navigating the Quadrants

Domain skills are the single most important activity
(they are the furthest to the right) C-level executives
consider when hiring or evaluating professional
services providers. But they are also on the bottom
half of the chart. Meaning, they are poor
differentiators—C-levels can usually find a firm with
the skills needed.

A Hard Pill to Swallow

Professionally, we are often most proud of our domain skills.
After all, we studied for at least 4 years to get our degrees and up
to 10 years to earn advanced degrees. We display them proudly
on our office walls. Then we spend another 8 to 10 years honing our abilities and building experience and perspective.

These highly developed skills are what define us in our
career. We want to talk about our talents. We are proud to regale
clients and potential clients with the depth of our abilities.

If you can't convince a client you have the domain skills

necessary for their work, it will mean an instant veto. However, having the skills a client is seeking will only earn you consideration to be hired. In short, your skills don't get you hired—they get you into consideration. End of story. Domain skills are a litmus test. Clients expect you to possess these talents.

Much like potty training, clients aren't too impressed when we tell them how well we can do our job. In fact, today's clients are more informed and connected than ever before and finding the expertise they need is a fairly painless process. A couple of phone calls to trusted colleagues and a few minutes on the Internet give C-level executives a short list of providers to consider. Every provider the client is considering will be able to do the job (at least, they have convinced the client they can do the job).

If every provider up for consideration has domain skills—and domain skills don't differentiate you from the competition—how do you convince clients you are the provider with whom they should invest their precious time and money?

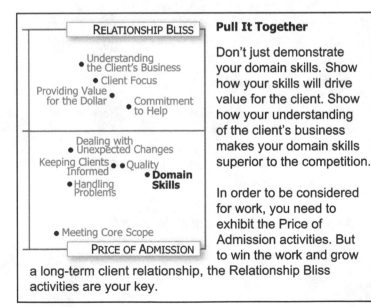

RELATIONSHIP BLISS

Understanding the Client's Business
• Client Focus
Providing Value for the Dollar
• Commitment to Help

Dealing with Unexpected Changes
Keeping Clients Informed • Quality
• Handling Problems • **Domain Skills**

• Meeting Core Scope

PRICE OF ADMISSION

Pull It Together

Don't just demonstrate your domain skills. Show how your skills will drive value for the client. Show how your understanding of the client's business makes your domain skills superior to the competition.

In order to be considered for work, you need to exhibit the Price of Admission activities. But to win the work and grow a long-term client relationship, the Relationship Bliss activities are your key.

Pulling It Together:

Leverage the Quadrants to Differentiate Expected Activities

Clients are only interested in how you will shape and apply your domain skills to their unique situations and idiosyncratic needs. The difference between simply validating your domain skills and demonstrating them in a client-centric manner is the difference between a lone professional looking for work and a flourishing client relationship.

Don't talk about yourself.

Whether you've been invited to respond to an RFP, participate in a pitch, or present to a hiring committee, you can make the same assumption: the client believes you can do the work. Your curriculum vitae, the founding history of your organization, and an overview presentation of the services you offer are no longer of interest. They've been to your website. Now they want to know what you're able to offer specific to their goals.

Cough up the great ideas.

If you aren't prepared to share a pointed piece of advice directly related to the client's unique situation, you aren't ready to meet with the client. At a minimum, do the research to show you understand the client, their business, products, industry, and competitive environment.

Arm yourself with smart questions.

The only way to demonstrate your understanding of the client's business (a Relationship Bliss activity) and their issues is to tell them. When a client doesn't need to educate you on their industry and general company information, you differentiate yourself much quicker. Ask probing questions to show you've done your homework ("In light of your recent acquisition of Company X, how will this project affect your integration efforts?"). Bring current, relevant data into the conversation ("2 weeks ago, Company Y did a soft launch of their newest product. As we discuss your objectives, we should keep this in mind").

Prepare to share.

Demonstrate the value your particular domain skills bring by sharing the practical insight you've gained from working with other clients in similar scenarios. Your ability to bring real-world experience to the client's situation is a differentiator.

- What lessons have you learned from dealing with these situations before?
- How can you use your past experience to ensure success in this particular case?
- What are the common pitfalls to expect—and how will you avoid them?
- How does this specific situation differ from what you've experienced in the past?

Listen more than you talk. A lot more.

Nuances, perspectives, underlying objectives, sensitivities; it's time to let the client do the talking so you can gather as much information as humanly possible to provide a truly tailored, client-focused solution. Clients almost always have secondary goals they are hoping to achieve. Learning—and meeting—all the objectives our clients have influences the way we approach the work. Be bold and ask the more sensitive questions. This

(continued on next page)

(continued from previous page)

will demonstrate you are invested in the project—and the relationship—more than simply completing the task at hand. You can start the conversation by asking:

- Tell me what you would like to achieve in order for the company to consider this project successful.
- What about for you, on a personal level? Is this tied to your compensation or any promotions?
- Who will be involved or watching the results of this project? Are there personalities, sensitivities, or relationships I should note?

Don't keep your best ideas to yourself.

Clients are seeking committed work partners. They want providers who are thinking about issues as frequently as they are. Whether you are in a pitch, a kick-off meeting, an annual review, or an impromptu meeting, always be prepared to share off-the-cuff strategies and ideas. The sooner you start talking about actual solutions, the closer you are to having new work. At worst, the client will not agree with your idea and you can brainstorm new solutions or understand their concerns better.

Bring clients into the process immediately.

Provide checklists and guidelines to help clients understand the process you are about to launch: timelines, an outline of key deliverables, FAQs, anything to help align their expectations to what you will deliver. This is a far more effective way to engage clients in your work than talking about all the things you plan to do. Show, don't tell.

CHAPTER 6

Quality

Quality Starts and Ends with Your Client

> *"Quality as a product or service is not what the supplier puts in. It is what the customer gets out and is willing to pay for. Customers pay only for what is of use to them and gives them value."*
>
> —PETER DRUCKER

The Outcome You Deliver Affects Your Client's Perception of Quality

LargeCorp, a leading specialty chemical company, needed to replace the existing wastewater capture system in one of its older, but highly profitable, plants. LargeCorp hired a world-class engineering firm, Quality Engineers, to help evaluate the situation.

The management of LargeCorp provided Quality Engineers with all the materials and documents needed to assemble the assessment: the leases for the property, detailed drawings showing the history of the existing wastewater capture system, and a complete record of every repair and update to the system since it was built. The engineers pored over the documents and studied the physical plant and system. After several months of detailed analyses, Quality Engineers had reached its conclusion.

A top officer of LargeCorp reviewed the initial recommendations. Quality Engineers had clearly assembled an extraordinarily detailed analysis. Quality Engineers was proud of their precise calculations and in-depth analysis, including the extensive discussion of potential solutions outlining the drawbacks and benefits of each. After walking LargeCorp through the analysis, Quality Engineers offered their final recommendation: a new system projected to last between 20 and 25 years. This option, while requiring a substantial initial investment, was the most cost-effective approach for LargeCorp over the long term based on maintenance and historical production levels, including peaks and valleys.

Unimpressed, LargeCorp informed Quality Engineers they would not be moving ahead with their recommendation. The engineers were confused and argued their case with LargeCorp, stressing the due diligence the engineers performed on their analysis and how their recommendation was based on an error-free calculation proving the solution dwarfed all others in terms of longevity and cost effectiveness over time. At this point, the officer of LargeCorp stated, "We are left questioning the judgment and true motivation behind your recommendation. If you had studied the lease and taken notes during the initial meeting, you would have realized LargeCorp only has 10 years left on a non-renewable lease. This property will be turned over to the county as part of an industrial development agreement. The system you are offering is clearly high quality, but you're offering us a limousine when a bicycle would work fine."

It doesn't matter how thorough or technically impressive a solutions is. If we fundamentally do not meet our clients' needs, we are doomed to failure. In the case of LargeCorp and Quality Engineers (a true story with the names changed to protect the guilty), Quality Engineers had an indisputable analysis. Unfortunately, their commitment to the process—not the client's needs—caused them to overlook a crucial client constraint. In this case, it was a costly (albeit high-quality) mistake.

Always ask yourself: Does my solution meet the client's needs? If it does, most transgressions are forgiven. If it doesn't, your quality is looked upon poorly—no matter how well thought out your solution—because you weren't client focused in your approach.

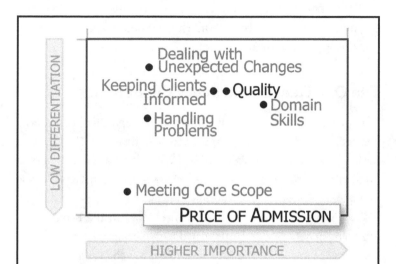

Navigating the Quadrants

Quality—like all of the activities in the lower-right quadrant—is expected, not respected, by clients. If a client questions your quality, be concerned.

Since the activities in this lower-right quadrant are more readily available, having a deficiency here will make you a prime target for replacement.

When is the last time a client asked to see your quality assurance processes? In the professional services world, few clients can (or want to) see your rigorous review and thorough work processes. Instead, clients build their perception of your quality around their experience with you.

Also, because you are in the service business, clients come to their conclusions based on their whole experience with you—not just the final product or service.

The One Deliverable Every Client Reads

Julian, a nationally renowned litigator and name partner in a law firm, was representing one of the largest banks in the world. The case was particularly thorny and high profile. Haylie, the bank's CFO, would often characterize the work as "watching a symphony" and "a fine opera."

3 years passed and the case was resolved to the bank's overwhelming benefit. The firm submitted a final invoice. Haylie scanned the invoice, looking for the total, and found it well into the 7 figures. Haylie put the 86-page document back in its envelope and placed the invoice on the credenza behind her desk.

Almost 4 months passed. Julian called Haylie and after some chit-chat Julian inquired about the status of payment. Haylie indicated she did not understand the invoice and could not pass it on to her CEO for approval. Julian asked what questions Haylie had and added, "You won handsomely."

Haylie indicated she could not accept the invoice. Julian asked why. Haylie replied she could not make heads or tails of the "impenetrable 86-page thicket of fog with thousands of random time entries." The invoice needs more information as to what the charges were for and why this time was incurred. She added, "This will never fly with my CEO." Julian said he "would look into it."

After 5 days of radio silence, Haylie called Julian. The famed partner replied: "My accounting department says we can't change the invoice or get more detail at this point." No apology, no explanation.

Haylie only half-jokingly suggested Julian do it himself as the bill would not be paid without meeting the guidelines. This firm received no new matters from the bank for years to follow.

One pivotal document managed to alienate two decision makers at a mega client. The CFO could not believe anyone was controlling the costs if the invoices were not organized and well presented. Good invoicing means good risk management and cost control. The invoice served as the last event the client remembered.

Of all the deliverables you give to your client throughout the life of a project, the invoice is the one they are guaranteed to read. Your invoice is a defining document representing you, your work product, and the way you manage the work process. There are few documents your clients will scrutinize as closely as your invoice.

Factual errors leave clients questioning the rigor and diligence in your work. Complex and hard-to-understand invoices imply a disorganized, inefficient work process. These are not the final impressions we want to leave with clients if we expect to be hired again.

Simple, easy-to-understand invoices represent clear and decisive work. Talk to the client about their preferences for how invoices are formatted. An inability to customize an invoice to meet the client's needs is perceived as dismissive of the relationship. Review the invoice directly with the client to demonstrate a commitment to the client and the relationship.

Clients Set Expectations of Quality Before You Begin the Work

Quality is assessed the very first time you speak with a potential client. C-level executives expect to see your best and most thoughtful work up front—after all, you are trying to win their dollars.

The expectation is you will walk in the door having performed enough due diligence and homework to begin discussing the specific issues at hand. Few things scream low quality louder than cookie-cutter approaches to pitches and responses to RFPs. Your ability to speak about substantive issues during a pitch or business development endeavor demonstrates quality. It shows an investment of time and a proactive approach others lack.

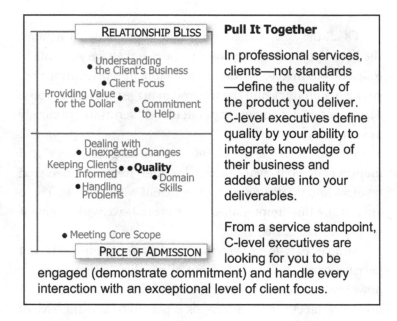

Pull It Together

In professional services, clients—not standards—define the quality of the product you deliver. C-level executives define quality by your ability to integrate knowledge of their business and added value into your deliverables.

From a service standpoint, C-level executives are looking for you to be engaged (demonstrate commitment) and handle every interaction with an exceptional level of client focus.

Pulling It Together:

Leverage the Quadrants to Differentiate Expected Activities

In my 25 years speaking with C-level executives, I've heard some stunning stories where one slip-up by a service provider submarined the client relationship because it made the client question the provider's overall quality. Many times, the slip-up was dismissed by the service provider as the interaction wasn't even part of the final deliverable, but was an essential part of the relationship.

Don't overlook everyday interactions.

For weeks on end, a junior-level account planner, Agnus, had been emailing the Director of Marketing and all of her direct reports at a large, well-known consumer goods manufacturer. Each email started with, "Dear Kerri" instead of "Kari"—the client's actual name. Agnus never caught her mistake despite Kari making a point of signing her name at the end of each email and including her signature line. Finally, after a month of correspondence, Kari took the blunt approach responding to one of Agnus' emails with, "Dear Anus, please check the spelling of my name before sending your next email to me and my department. You can see how embarrassing it is when someone gets your name wrong. Thanks, Kari."

Few things pierce a client's heart as swiftly as errors or mistakes. Clients have amazing patience, but consistent typos or more substantive data errors tend to deflate even the most understanding of clients. Correct, complete, current, and consistent information is expected. Sloppy work translates into sloppy approaches and lack of focus. Clients will interpret a mistake-laden deliverable as your lack of commitment to them and their goals.

CHAPTER 7

Meeting Core Scope

Manage Scope to Manage the Relationship

Joan, the Chief Marketing Officer (CMO) at a Fortune 500 company, engaged Insightful Web Design to design a website for a new consumer product. This high-profile product was the first in a new product line scheduled to be rolled out over the next 18 months. The product line had its own budget; the line was being watched at the highest levels of the company.

Exactly 26 days before the scheduled live date, Joan called Zack, the partner at Insightful Web Design. Joan informed Zack the company had decided to sell the product directly from the website, an idea Joan had originally resisted. Zack smiled inside and out knowing he had won a small victory in helping his client.

Zack marshaled the team and planned for the ambitious task of adding a fully-tested ecommerce platform by the launch date. Zack added staff and brought in a couple of contractors. The work days expanded to 12 and then 18 hours. This was a robust effort and Zack was not going to fail. Zack had grand visions of building the web presence for the rest of the product line.

After much wear and tear, the fully functional website launched on time with a robust ecommerce capability. Customers were buying the new product from the site in droves.

About 45 days later Joan called Zack. "I'm confused," said Joan. The invoice for the site was 22% over the fixed budget. "Those are the extra charges for the ecommerce platform," said Zack. He explained how much work was needed to meet the deadlines to ensure the ecommerce portion went live at launch.

"I had no idea the cost would be this much. Why didn't you tell me? Everyone is watching the budget on this. Everyone. I now have to go begging for the money hat-in-hand. Why didn't you tell me?" Joan asked, almost incredulously.

Zack had never explained the ecommerce addition meant a change in scope. Joan said, "If the ecommerce costs were extra, I needed to know when we decided to sell from the site—so I could let people know—and look like I have a handle on this. Now I look like an idiot." Everyone in the company was watching her project. Joan did not think about the additional costs the changes to the scope caused by the new work. Zack could have saved the day by quoting a fee for the work early in the process.

Changes in scope either create or destroy value. Zack saw a chance for adding value only to see it become a costly overrun. Not the intent—but surely the result.

WHENEVER I AM GIVING A TALK ON THE 17 ACTIVITIES, I ASK the crowd a question as I start to discuss scope.

"By a show of hands, how many people in the room have had a client change their mind throughout the course of a project?"

Virtually everyone shoots a hand up into the air. The point being, scope is a constantly moving target.

Intrinsically, the scope is a professional services firm's most important tool. Your scope establishes the expectations and boundaries of the work to be provided. However, scope can derail our best efforts if we aren't careful. The danger lies in how we communicate scope and scope changes to clients. Much like in the previous chapter on quality, you only meet scope if your client feels as though you met their goals. And, as my question to the audience shows, these goals change all the time. Your challenge is to keep up.

Once embedded in the actual work of a project, we tend to take scope for granted. We become lax in our communication regarding scope. We are focused on getting the job done and worry about the details at the end once we've delivered what the client wanted.

Suddenly scope becomes the enemy instead of a valued tool.

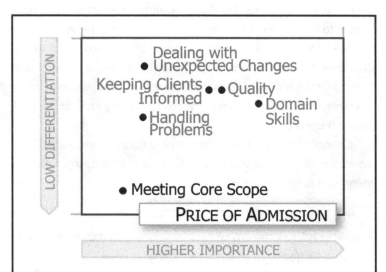

Navigating the Quadrants

Most professional services firms are expert at developing and meeting scope. Few mistakes sour a relationship quicker than not completing what you said you would. BTI's research shows C-level executives find this attribute widely available in their professional services firms.

Meeting the core scope is the minimum requirement. You can use scope to add value (identify key changes and communicate the implications with clients) or destroy value (overrun budget or timelines with little input from the client).

Surrender to the inevitable. The scope of a project will change somewhere along the way. New facts arise (or clients forget to give us all the information up front). Objectives change. Things happen.

As professionals, a scope-of-work document is a powerful tool to keep the client informed of changes—and more importantly, the impact of these changes on timing, budget and deliverables. Many times, we (wrongly) presume the client understands how changes they request will impact timing or budget.

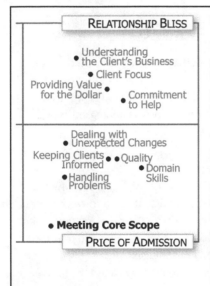

RELATIONSHIP BLISS	**Pull It Together**

Understanding the Client's Business • Client Focus • Providing Value for the Dollar • Commitment to Help

Dealing with • Unexpected Changes • Keeping Clients Informed • • Quality • Domain • Handling Problems Skills

• **Meeting Core Scope**

PRICE OF ADMISSION

Pull It Together

Transform scope into a productive communication tool for you to articulate your commitment, client focus, and value.

Think of your scope as a living document. As changes arise or new requests come in from the client, update the scope. Outline how these new circumstances impact the project (particularly as it relates to budget, staffing or timing).

Clients hate surprises. They hate surprises the most when they show up in the final invoice. Using a scope document to proactively communicate changes in scope and how they impact budget, timing, and deliverables is critical in maintaining a superior client relationship.

Pulling It Together:

Leverage the Quadrants to Differentiate Expected Activities

While this isn't a chapter on crafting a scope-of-work document or managing project work, there are ways to position the fundamentals of scope to ensure you are delivering on the Relationship Bliss activities.

The only valid goal is the client's goal.

Clear, concise objectives need to be built into a scope-of-work document. The goal guides every action and decision needed to complete a project. Be sure to actively confirm this goal with the client—in writing—before beginning any work.

Don't let the client question you.

You are the expert on how to get the job done. It's why the client hired you. However, it's important to go through your methodology with the client and align their expectations for your process. This helps avoid second-guessing and nit-picking when it comes time to pay the invoice.

At the onset of a project, outline and discuss the following with clients:

- Staffing mix
- Tasks and milestones
- Deliverables
- Your recommended approach and alternative approaches—be sure to discuss the implications of each possible approach and why you are suggesting your recommendation

The client has a role—an important one.

Most scope documents include a section on roles and responsibilities. Identify—by name, if possible—the key individuals working on a project and the role they will play. Delineate the decision makers, contact information, and an organizational chart. Do not forget to include the client and their role in the process you are about to undertake.

One tool to rule them all.

A well-built timeline can singlehandedly manage most issues regarding scope. The best timelines are based on duration and project events rather than calendar dates. This approach allows you to communicate the interdependencies of work tasks.

Event-driven: "Task A will be completed 2 weeks from approval by client."

Calendar-driven: "Task A will be completed by November 24th."

An event-driven timeline is a client-friendly vehicle to articulate the impact an action (or more likely inaction) will have on the targeted deliverable dates. Clients are able to see directly how their participation affects the timeline of the project. Build key decision points, needed approvals, client and vendor deliverables, and significant meetings into the timeline.

Just the facts.

A scope document is an opportunity to lay out your understanding of the facts regarding a project. Outlining how your approach is tied to key assumptions and facts gives the client the chance to correct any misinformation. Additionally, you may find a need to return to the facts when you discuss (inevitable) changes in scope and/or budget.

CHAPTER 8

Keeping Clients Informed

No News Is Bad News

WHY DIDN'T YOU CALL?

Picture your 16-year-old self. You are coming home late at night. Well past your curfew—think hours past your curfew. You head up to the front door. You brace yourself for the inevitable inquisition. The door knob is turning and your mother is already mid-sentence, "Where were you? I thought you were dead on the side of the road! Why didn't you call?" This is an early lesson on keeping clients informed.

Clients (like our dear mothers) will immediately jump to the worst conclusion possible. If you have been out of touch with a client at any point in a project, they begin to imagine all kinds of possible red flag scenarios from a disastrous outcome to a basic lack of investment from you. When the communication opens up again, it's too late. Ultimately the client is left feeling disappointed with your lack of proactive information: "Why didn't you call?"

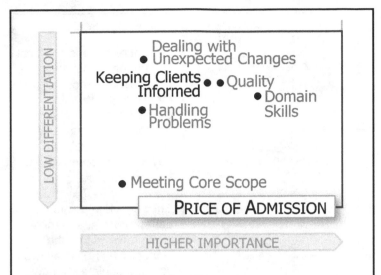

LOW DIFFERENTIATION

Dealing with
• Unexpected Changes
Keeping Clients • • Quality
Informed • Domain
• Handling Skills
Problems

• Meeting Core Scope

PRICE OF ADMISSION

HIGHER IMPORTANCE

Navigating the Quadrants

Clients expect to be informed throughout a project: progress, lack of progress, unexpected circumstances, or changes. Regular, proactive communication is the standard they anticipate.

Failure to keep your clients informed cracks at the foundation of client service and erodes relationships.

The challenge with this particular activity is figuring out exactly how frequently each client wants to hear from you. It's a fine line between over- and under-communicating. Some clients want to be deeply involved with daily (or more frequent) updates. Others are more hands-off, requiring only weekly or biweekly check-ins. Pick the wrong one and you will find yourself with a disgruntled client. There is only one way to know for sure: Ask.

The most effective scope-of-work document (Chapter 7) includes detailing the frequency of communication each client prefers.

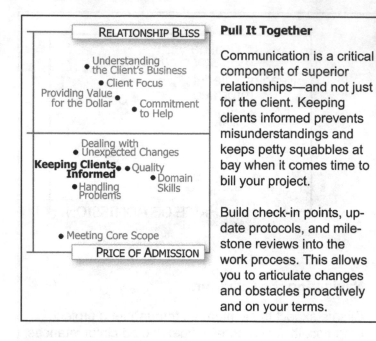

Pull It Together

Communication is a critical component of superior relationships—and not just for the client. Keeping clients informed prevents misunderstandings and keeps petty squabbles at bay when it comes time to bill your project.

Build check-in points, up-date protocols, and mile-stone reviews into the work process. This allows you to articulate changes and obstacles proactively and on your terms.

Pulling It Together:

Leverage the Quadrants to Differentiate Expected Activities

Effective communication is a cornerstone of building the strongest client relationships. At the core of every activity in the Clientelligence Matrix is communicating and demonstrating your ability to the client. However, all professional services firms are talking to their clients (presumably). In order to make you and your firm stand out, every communication you have with your client should prove your prowess in one of the Relationship Bliss activities.

Be responsive.

We are well past the mantras of "answer your phone in 3 rings" and "call your client back within 24 hours." While good rules of thumb, these do not embody the level of client focus your clients expect. Clients are seeking trusted partners— professional services firms able to understand exactly what keeps them up at night and what information is critical. In short, clients want someone who thinks like they do. While not a comprehensive list, my research shows professional services firms are most unresponsive in the following areas. Focusing on these areas for routine client check-ins will set you apart:

- *Confirmation of client objectives.* I discuss this in the previous chapter on scope, but it bears repeating. Confirming client objectives—in writing—is mission critical when starting a project. A misunderstanding, incomplete information, or a shift in client thinking can and usually does set a project on the wrong course. It's up to you to ask the right questions to make

(continued on next page)

(continued from previous page)

sure both you and the client are on the same page at the start—and throughout the lifecycle—of a project. What is the outcome you want from this effort?

> How will you measure success?
> How will you be using this work product?
> What will management expect of you?
> How does this project play into the overall goals and strategic direction of your business?

• *Changes in billing.* If something is going to impact the price or budget estimate of a project, the client wants to know, no matter how trivial. This includes any changing in staffing. Don't let the invoice be the first place where a client sees the name of someone who worked on their project.

On a related note, don't assume the client will understand their impact on the budget. Clients change their minds, they ask for new deliverables, or they need the project to wrap a month earlier than originally scheduled. Proactively discuss how these changes will affect the final budget. Clients are quick to forget how they changed scope, but quicker to remember how you changed the price.

• *Generic observations vs. pointed recommendations.* The epitome of client focus is providing your client with a direct piece of information specific to their company. It demonstrates you understand the client and their business.

No matter what service you provide, clients hired you to help guide their company—not give a generic, cookie-cutter dissertation on facts. Clients will read your communications only if they offer a pointed piece of advice or recommendation directly related to your client. And don't be afraid to take a stance. Clients will tell you if they don't agree, but they have more confidence in providers who don't couch their recommendations. Try the following statements on for size:

> Given Company Y's goal of reducing costs, I would

recommend Option 1. Option 2 is also viable, but it costs 3 times as much.

> While the overall manufacturing industry is facing regulatory pressure, the unique qualities of Product Z indicate this is a good time to launch.

Informal communications drive the best relationships.

Check-ins are a necessity, but engaging the client on a more personal level demonstrates your commitment to the client and leads the way to broader relationships. We frequently get caught up in formal project communications, ignoring our client on a more personal level. After sending the formal communication, take a moment to follow up with your direct contact in an informal manner (email or phone works great).

- How do you feel the project is going?
- Is the progress of the project to date measuring up to your vision?
- What has the reaction to the project been from elsewhere in your company?
- What information or reporting styles would make it easier for you to communicate within your company?

Come clean early.

Mistakes happen. Deadlines are missed. Budgets are blown. Take the proactive approach with your client rather than hoping they won't notice. They will. Once a project gets off track, set up a time to talk with the client. Be prepared with the following:

- *An apology.* It's a forgotten art and is the first step at diffusing the situation. Apologize and get on to fixing the issue.

(continued on next page)

(continued from previous page)

- *High-level summary of the issue.* There's no time (and it's unprofessional) to assign blame or detail how everything went wrong. Provide a quick synopsis of the issue and how you plan on solving it.
- *Impacts.* Lay out the facts on how the issue will change the original scope (budget, timeline, outcome).
- *Recommendations.* Let the client know your plan for moving forward to keep to the original scope as closely as possible. Reassure the client how you have taken steps to ensure this problem will not occur again.
- *Ask your client.* Have an open discussion with your client on their preferences and priorities in light of the new circumstances. Sometimes objectives will change based on the magnitude of the issue. Give your client the chance to be part of the solution so they know what they need to communicate back to their management.

CHAPTER 9

Dealing with Unexpected Changes

Adaptation not Preparation

> *You can't stop the waves, but you can learn to surf.*
>
> —JON KABAT-ZINN

After a long, expensive battle, ad agency ABC finally won and signed a $1.6 million deal with consumer goods giant, Company T. The work was slated to cover a number of channels and campaigns. After a brief celebration, agency ABC got to work.

A month into the project, Company T met with the leadership of agency ABC and informed them of a new budget cap placed on the organization as a whole. The new budget allotted to marketing was $1 million. No exceptions.

Budget changes are a way of life in advertising—and almost any professional services company—so agency ABC enacted their usual process: reassess scope, outline recommendations, meet with the client, gain approval on new scope, and get back to work.

The new scope of work was approved by Company T and work resumed. In light of Company T's new budget restraints, agency ABC decided to meet monthly with Company T in order to provide budget updates to aid the client in their new reporting process.

Agency ABC used these meetings to discuss the budget, but conversations would cover the work to date, and on a more general basis, how Company T's marketing department was handling the new budget constraints and its impact on their goals. It was during one of these meetings where Company T's CMO mentioned a small project he had hoped to get off the ground was shelved until funds became available. Agency ABC used this information to put together a budget and timeline for the project for when Company T was ready to move forward on it.

A month later, at the next budget meeting, the CMO awarded the project to agency ABC saying, "This budget was just the tool I needed to talk to my CEO. We both agreed on the strategic importance of the project and the budget was slightly less than what we thought it would cost."

Throughout the lifecycle of the original project, new small projects continued to come to life due to agency ABC's commitment and client focus.

By the end of the year, agency ABC had billed $2.1 million to Company T—$500,000 more than the original budget and $1.1 million more than the revised budget—and Company T was happy to pay every penny.

CONSTANT CHANGE IS THE REALITY OF BUSINESS. IT'S WHY ONE of the most frequent pieces of advice business leaders share is: be prepared for anything. I would like to offer up a more precise variation on this advice: be prepared to adapt.

We can't anticipate exactly what will change as we begin working on a project, so preparing for all potential scenarios isn't effective—or efficient. What we do know is something will change and change—like all other obstacles we face in business—can be managed. The best approach is to prepare how we will respond to changes when they arise.

Clients hire us for our experience. It's their unwritten insurance policy for when the unforeseen takes place. Clients find comfort in our ability to leverage past experiences and knowledge to their benefit. Experience benefits us as well. Our experience helps inform us on the changes we can most likely expect throughout a project.

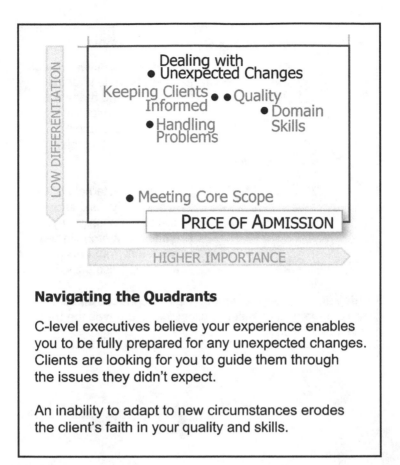

LOW DIFFERENTIATION

Dealing with
• Unexpected Changes
Keeping Clients • • Quality
Informed   • Domain
• Handling   Skills
Problems

• Meeting Core Scope

PRICE OF ADMISSION

HIGHER IMPORTANCE

Navigating the Quadrants

C-level executives believe your experience enables you to be fully prepared for any unexpected changes. Clients are looking for you to guide them through the issues they didn't expect.

An inability to adapt to new circumstances erodes the client's faith in your quality and skills.

But don't get overconfident. First, many professional services firms come touting experience similar to our own. Second, something new will always manage to shake things up in a different way.

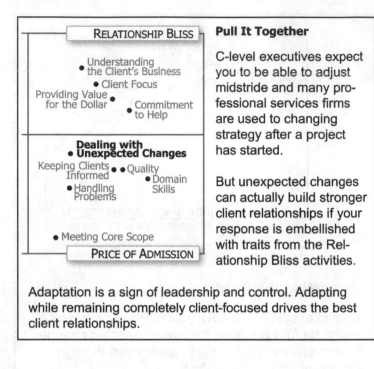

Pull It Together

C-level executives expect you to be able to adjust midstride and many professional services firms are used to changing strategy after a project has started.

But unexpected changes can actually build stronger client relationships if your response is embellished with traits from the Relationship Bliss activities.

Adaptation is a sign of leadership and control. Adapting while remaining completely client-focused drives the best client relationships.

Pulling It Together:

Leverage the Quadrants to Differentiate Expected Activities

Embracing, instead of fighting, unexpected changes can be a useful tool when building the best client relationships. C-levels executives look to work with providers able to manage issues and navigate murky waters, all while still delivering the outcome the client wants to achieve.

Dealing with Change

Step 1: STOP

Many times when something changes on us, our instinct is to respond; to quickly adjust our approach to minimize impact. Don't trust your instincts just yet. Clients want to understand the nature of the change and the potential impact before pursuing a new course of action. Projects typically impact multiple areas within a client's organization and your client is going to want to assess all the potential impacts before moving forward.

Step 2: Assess

For everyone's benefit—yours and the client's—when a significant change occurs, it's always best to reassess scope. The majority of clients will want to know how a change will impact:

- Outcome
- Timing
- Risk exposure

- Budget
- Staffing

(continued on next page)

(continued from previous page)

Step 3: Report and revise

Once you've outlined the change and its impact on the project, it's time to meet with the client. Provide a high-level view of the issue and outline your recommendation. Then let the client do the talking. Clients need to be involved in the final decision for their peace of mind—and yours.

Step 4: Get back to work

CHAPTER 10

Handling Problems

Your Problem Is Your Problem

Leonard, a senior litigator, was representing his longtime client, Mega-Pharm, a large pharmaceutical company. MegaPharm was being sued in connection with a marquee product. Leonard reviewed the documentation and started planning the process of defending his client, as he had for 16 years. Leonard mapped out a plan and had his team do some preliminary work. The strategy—defend at the lowest possible cost.

Gina, the Chief Legal Officer at MegaPharm, asked Leonard for an update so she could brief her CEO. MegaPharm had a relatively new CEO in his 14th month into the job. Leonard reviewed his plan and work to date—proud of his ability to be fully in control of the matter.

Gina looked at Leonard and asked "How much are we into this so far?"

"About $110,000, give or take," Leonard responded. Gina asked where he was headed—Leonard explained some legal maneuvers which clearly pointed to a defense which would defend the company but keep costs low.

"Leonard, our new CEO is all about keeping the bad news and combative behavior out of the public eye—he thinks it's bad for the stock price. Besides, this is our marquis product—it's the goose that laid the golden egg. Bury this somewhere so it doesn't get noticed any more than it is."

The game had changed. New CEOs often mean new objectives. Leonard was a person who always knew his client—until the rules changed. The lesson: always confirm your client's objectives no matter how obvious they seem or how well you know your client.

HANDLING PROBLEMS IS THE MORE TROUBLESOME COUSIN TO dealing with unexpected changes (discussed in detail in the previous chapter). So why aren't these 2 activities rolled into one? There are 2 distinctions between unexpected changes and problems:

- Problems are always bad.
- A problem arises as a result of something YOU (not the client) did—or didn't—do.

Mistakes happen. At some point in a project, you or someone on your team will make a mistake. There are 3 options to consider:

1. Avoid telling the client—and get as creative as possible for putting off client conversations.
2. Cover your butt immediately.
3. Take accountability and tell the client immediately.

At this stage in our careers, we know all the reasons why options 1 and 2 are inappropriate. So, we are left with option 3: take accountability and tell the client (almost) immediately. But before we can fall on our sword, we need to be prepared with a direction to move forward. Being able to propose steps to help solve the problem prevents a flesh wound from becoming a mortal blow (to the client relationship).

I hope you picked up on my careful choice of wording above. I did not say you need to present the solution to the problem when you approach your client. You need the direction and options for moving forward. Somewhere along the way, the same people who said you must answer a phone

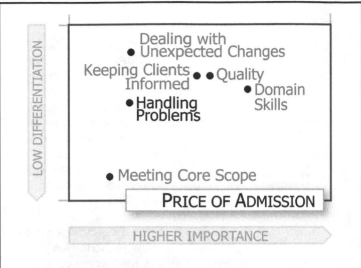

LOW DIFFERENTIATION

Dealing with
● Unexpected Changes
Keeping Clients ● ● Quality
Informed ● Domain
● Handling Skills
Problems

● Meeting Core Scope

PRICE OF ADMISSION

HIGHER IMPORTANCE

Navigating the Quadrants

C-level executives want you to be professional
enough to acknowledge a problem—and be
prepared to present a path for moving forward.
They expect accountability and action.

Clients do not want your problem to become
their problem.

within 3 rings made up the rule saying you must have the solution before approaching a client with a problem.

The underlying thesis is correct: do not make the client solve your problem. The execution is completely faulty. You only need a skeleton of a solution to start. You are usually better served bringing multiple ideas for solutions to your client. Presenting multiple solutions helps bring your client into the process and offers them a sense of ownership.

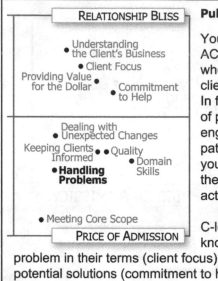

Pull It Together

You do not need the ACTUAL solution in hand when you approach your client to discuss a problem. In fact, offering a handful of potential solutions and engaging the client in the path moving forward is your way of introducing the Relationship Bliss activities.

C-level executives want to know you're thinking of the problem in their terms (client focus), have come up with potential solutions (commitment to help), and are considering the potential impact on them and their organization (understanding the client's business).

Pulling It Together:

Leverage the Quadrants to Differentiate Expected Activities

Be solution-oriented, not solution-focused.

Failure to include the client in the final decision on how to rectify the problem could potentially undermine your relationship. C-level executives continually tell me one of the top issues driving them crazy is when a professional services provider makes a decision without their authorization.

Save the story-telling for happy hour.

Cliffhangers and drawn-out woven tales of intrigue. No one has time for the story of how a problem came to be. C-level executives are looking for immediate, succinct communication regarding a problem. No sugar-coating, no slow dancing around the issue. State problems in a clear, concise manner. The sooner solutions are discussed, the better. Immediacy gives clients the opportunity to manage their own internal organization. Problems—particularly ones impacting scope or budget—have a funny way of finding their way to the CEO or CFO.

Take the bullet and move on.

Blame. This is a topic of great interest in the business world. We know it is unprofessional to assign blame for a problem, so a new word was created to make it more digestible: accountability. "I don't blame you, but I hold you accountable."

Issues need to be owned in the business world. We know the reason why something failed. It's how we ultimately improve processes and weed out ineffective ideas

(continued on next page)

(continued from previous page)

(and sometimes individuals). However, the time to assign "accountability" is not in the heat of facing a problem.

We can only work towards solutions after there is ownership of a problem—so take ownership immediately—yes, you—to start the problem-solving process. (We'll discuss how to ensure the problem doesn't stick to you in a moment.)

Be detailed about the impact—not the problem.

C-level executives do not have the patience to listen to an entire saga of how a problem came to exist, but they do want to understand exactly how the problem will affect them professionally and personally. In short, what's the damage assessment? Be prepared to openly and honestly discuss how the problem impacts:

- Budget
- Timing
- Outcomes
- Organizational perceptions
- Risk exposure

Present your solution—then listen.

Work with your client and the project delivery team to determine the best course of action. Determining what is in the best interest of the project—and the client—is central to this planning process. The client's input provides full insight into their underlying motivations.

Tie up loose ends.

You've solved the problem, but don't let the conversation end there. Perform a post-project review with your team—and with the client—to bring full closure and eliminate any lingering concerns the client may have.

(continued on next page)

- Start on the upbeat: what went well with the project?
- Lead the conversation on what went wrong—don't let the client bring up the issues—then you're playing defense when you want to play offense
  - > As part of this conversation, detail the steps you are taking to ensure future issues of this nature will be avoided
- Ensure the overall client objectives were met regardless of the path taken to get there

WRAP-UP

Quadrant II
The Price of Admission

IF YOU CAN'T BRING THE BASICS, A CLIENT WILL NOT EVEN entertain the notion of entering into a relationship with you. At a minimum, you need to prove your ability to perform in each of these 6 areas. However, filtering in behaviors from the Relationship Bliss quadrant will help you leverage these core requirements into the foundation of a solid client relationship.

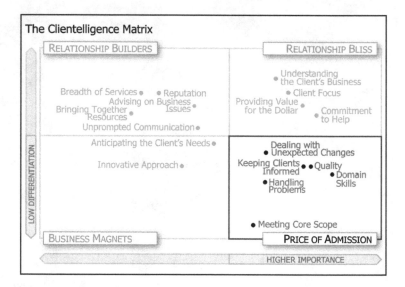

The Clientelligence Matrix

RELATIONSHIP BUILDERS

RELATIONSHIP BLISS

Breadth of Services • • Reputation
Advising on Business Issues •
Bringing Together • Resources
Unprompted Communication •

Understanding • the Client's Business
• Client Focus
Providing Value • for the Dollar
• Commitment to Help

Anticipating the Client's Needs •

Innovative Approach •

Dealing with • Unexpected Changes
Keeping Clients • • Quality Informed
• Domain
• Handling Skills Problems

• Meeting Core Scope

LOW DIFFERENTIATION

BUSINESS MAGNETS

PRICE OF ADMISSION

HIGHER IMPORTANCE

QUADRANT III

Relationship Builders

5 Niceties—Not Necessities

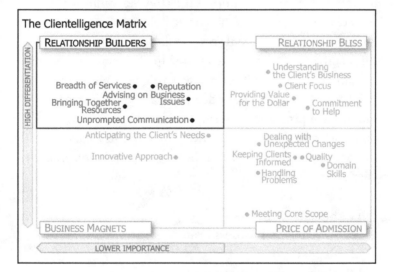

The Clientelligence Matrix

RELATIONSHIP BUILDERS — RELATIONSHIP BLISS

HIGH DIFFERENTIATION

Breadth of Services ● ● Reputation
Advising on Business ●
Bringing Together ● Issues ●
Resources
Unprompted Communication ●

Understanding
● the Client's Business
● Client Focus
Providing Value ●
for the Dollar ● Commitment
to Help

Anticipating the Client's Needs ●

Innovative Approach ●

Dealing with
● Unexpected Changes
Keeping Clients ● ● Quality
Informed ● Domain
● Handling Skills
Problems

● Meeting Core Scope

BUSINESS MAGNETS — PRICE OF ADMISSION

LOWER IMPORTANCE

Relationship Builders:
Lower Importance / Higher Differentiation

The 5 Relationship Builder activities, located on the top-half of the chart, provide a high degree of differentiation for professional services firms. With few professional services firms able to offer these 5 traits, the ability to deliver these helps you outpace competitors—winning you more work and more loyal clients.

However—and this is a big however—Relationship Builder activities are located on the left side of the chart, meaning they are less important (but not unimportant) to C-level executives. These activities help sustain relationships, but are only nice to have if you also deliver on the Relationship Bliss activities. Without Relationship Bliss, clients see Relationship Builder activities as distracting and one-note.

An air of caution around these 5 activities is needed. Too often, I see professional services firms focusing their energy on these activities instead of Relationship Bliss activities only to find they are unable to sustain long-term relationships with clients:

11. Breadth of Services
12. Advising on Business Issues
13. Reputation
14. Unprompted Communication
15. Bringing Together Resources

CHAPTER 11

Breadth of Services

Jack of All Trades, Master of All

> *"I wish there were more people at Firm Y who I had the relationship with and confidence in that I have with my primary contact. They seem a little thin in the ranks in transactional work."*
> —Chief Financial Officer, Global Bank on their
> Big 4 Accounting Firm

> *"They haven't told me about or marketed themselves to us. I have no idea what else they do."*
> —Business Director, Major Manufacturer on their
> Global Marketing Agency

Offering a wide breadth of services is an advantage for all. From the provider's standpoint, it's all about cross-selling. More services equal more revenue. From the client's standpoint, they have fewer providers to manage, spend less time educating outsiders on their organization, and have a full-service provider who can bring a holistic view and approach to the work.

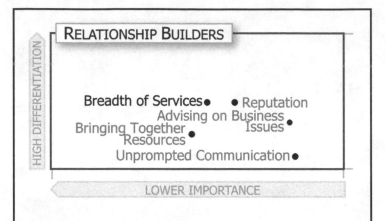

HIGH DIFFERENTIATION

Breadth of Services● ● Reputation
Advising on Business
Bringing Together ● Issues ●
Resources ●
Unprompted Communication ●

LOWER IMPORTANCE

Navigating the Quadrants

Finding a firm able to offer a strong breadth of
services is viewed as a luxury by clients. Few
firms are able to demonstrate the highest levels
of expertise and experience across more than 2
or 3 core service areas.

Long-term relationships are built on a professional
services provider's ability to leverage knowledge
of a client organization across services. Success
demands uniformity in the quality of work products
and single-stream management.

Despite a host of advantages, the overwhelming majority
of C-level executives purchase an average of 1.2 services from
their professional services providers. Those with the best relationships buy 3.2 services. The issue, however, is rarely with
the provider's capability. Instead, C-level executives say other
individuals within the professional services firm aren't introduced in a manner inspiring trust or building value.

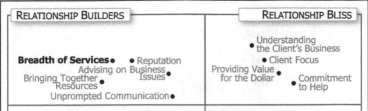

RELATIONSHIP BUILDERS	RELATIONSHIP BLISS
Breadth of Services • • Reputation Advising on Business • Bringing Together • Issues • Resources • Unprompted Communication •	• Understanding the Client's Business • Client Focus Providing Value • for the Dollar • Commitment to Help

Pull It Together

Effectively showcasing your breadth of services requires more than telling clients about your capabilities and making introductions to others within your firm. To truly build up your client relationships, a deep understanding of the client's business coupled with unwavering commitment to helping them is the only way to build trust and make the client see value in using your firm in multiple areas.

Pulling It Together:

Leverage the Quadrants to Build the Strongest Relationships

Make clients love your business development calls.

It's a discussion every client-facing professional has at some point in their career: understanding the types of work they outsource, you tell your client about how your firm provides Service B, in addition to Service A, which is already being delivered. "Oh, we already have someone in place with whom we are quite happy, but I'll let you know if something comes up." The conversation is dead before it gets started.

C-level executives don't have time to listen to spiels, unsolicited, generic pitches, or a laundry list of services you provide. To break through the noise of hundreds (sometimes thousands) of other providers and win time with key decision makers, you need to solve their problem before they hire you. You can read the last sentence again—it won't change. Before a client pays you, do the work.

Approaching a client by discussing an actual, specific issue their organization is facing—and coming armed with a potential solution—is an attention-getter. This technique draws on each of the 4 Relationship Bliss activities:

- You've shown you understand the client's business
- You are prepared—and committed—to helping solve the issue
- Immediately you are proving the value you can bring to the situation by leveraging your knowledge of the client
- And (unlike the countless other firms discussing their services and expertise) your client-focused approach will make you stand apart from the crowd

Winning additional work is one-third of the battle; keeping the work is the rest.

Make it easy for clients to use you. It sounds simple, but all too frequently professional services providers default to what's easy from their own client management standpoint.

- *Training and education is your responsibility*
  When clients turn to a professional services firm for multiple service areas, they expect the same level of knowledge about the business and industry from everyone. Instead, most clients find little coordination within their professional services providers and are left repeating the same information to multiple individuals within a single firm—frustrating and inefficient for busy C-level executives.

  Combat this by hosting internal meetings with any provider in your firm who is working at the same client organization—regardless of their discipline. During these meetings, discuss the breadth of work currently being covered—both the nuances of each project and how it fits into the overall goals of the client organization. This is the time to share client preferences and expectations so the entire team is ready to best serve the client.
- *Enthusiasm goes a long way*
  There is a natural enthusiasm generated when faced with the prospect of building a new relationship. When new team members from a single firm are introduced to the client, it is rare to see the same level of enthusiasm. There is a lower level of risk perceived—so less adrenaline-driven enthusiasm—since the relationship is technically already in place.

  The challenge here is when C-level executives meet your competitors. Competitors often bring a high level of enthusiasm to the client's work because they are trying to build a new relationship. Excitement and enthusiasm

(continued on next page)

(continued from previous page)

are contagious. Make sure clients catch it from you and not another provider.

- *One point of contact to rule them all*
No matter how many services a client purchases from you, clients want one—and only one—person leading the team and being accountable. Serving a client successfully across multiple areas requires a high, uniform standard be met in every area. Your original relationship built client expectations—and confidence—around your work product. Clients presume they will have similar experiences across your service offerings. Uniform delivery and single-stream leadership are seen as great benefits to clients and alleviate concerns of inconsistency across multiple service areas.

    If the client lead is not obvious, invite client feedback on the choice of primary contact. They will pick the individual they most want to interact with on a routine basis.

CHAPTER 12

Advising on Business Issues
The Vendor or the Mentor?

A leading, global corporate law firm, accustomed to working with large organizations, found itself pitching a well-known consumer products manufacturer. This manufacturer produced goods which were better known than the company itself.

The savvy law firm knew they needed to convince the manufacturer of their attorneys' depth of knowledge and understanding of the industry. On the day of the pitch, the law firm made observations on the marketplace and shared a pointed piece of advice the law firm was quite proud of, "While you are the dominant player in this market, there is a potential flaw in your business strategy. Your numerous acquisitions are beginning to draw harsh criticism from your competitors. This typically leads to harmful lawsuits and irreparable reputational damage."

The law firm, feeling quite pleased with how well they brought business insight into the conversation, continued, "Luckily, we have identified the competitor most likely to bring about such damage and some strategies you can take to protect your organization." The next slide in the presentation unveiled the logo of the "enemy."

The manufacturer looked at the law firm and quietly replied, "I assure you this competitor will not cause us any harm. This competitor, which you have singled out, has been acquired by us not 18 months ago—and we adhere to a strict policy of not allowing one division to sue another."

The manufacturer rose, expressed appreciation for the law firm's time and energy, and wished them the best of luck as the meeting ended earlier than expected.

HELPING CLIENTS BY OFFERING TARGETED BUSINESS ADVICE IS a proven differentiator and relationship builder—when it's done properly.

It is becoming increasingly difficult to differentiate on expertise alone (see Domain Skills, Chapter 5). The speed with which information is shared in today's business environment makes basic knowledge a commodity. Want to know the latest regulations impacting your organization? There's a dedicated website you can visit. Need in-depth analytics to understand your digital marketing penetration? Google can get you the information in minutes. Looking to streamline workflow or implement business process improvements? A quick Internet search yields more than 8 million hits providing step-by-step guides. Unless you bring more than expertise to the table, C-level executives will consider you just another vendor.

Through the course of our research, one of the more common complaints we hear from clients—even ones in close relationships with their service providers—is the lack of business-oriented advice they receive from external professionals. Although a sore point, clients are quick to acknowledge, "Providing business advice isn't something we ask of our professional services providers."

While they aren't outright asking for business advice, my research indicates this strategic positioning is valued and sought out by clients.

C-level executives, in particular, want unequivocal recommendations on actions, strategies, and solutions—and they want to know exactly how your recommendations will impact their business. Making a recommendation means sticking your neck out, but it also means you are committed to helping

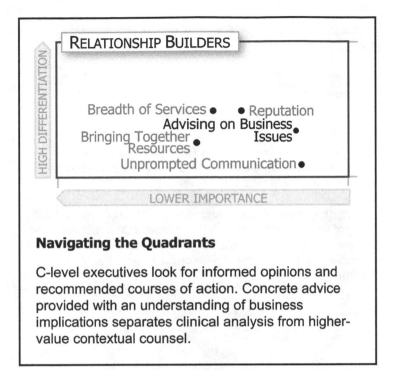

RELATIONSHIP BUILDERS

HIGH DIFFERENTIATION

Breadth of Services ●   ● Reputation
Advising on Business ●
Bringing Together ●   **Issues** ●
Resources ●
Unprompted Communication ●

LOWER IMPORTANCE

Navigating the Quadrants

C-level executives look for informed opinions and recommended courses of action. Concrete advice provided with an understanding of business implications separates clinical analysis from higher-value contextual counsel.

your client—rather than offering a clinical observation for the client to act upon.

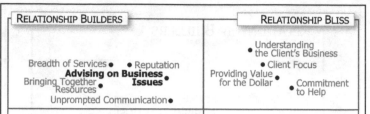

RELATIONSHIP BUILDERS	RELATIONSHIP BLISS
Breadth of Services • • Reputation **Advising on Business** • Bringing Together • **Issues** Resources Unprompted Communication •	• Understanding the Client's Business • Client Focus Providing Value • for the Dollar • • Commitment to Help

Pull It Together

The inextricable link between Relationship Builders and Relationship Bliss is clear as you analyze what is needed to provide advice on business issues.

Targeted, relevant advice demands a thorough understanding of your client's business. Your advice demonstrates you have a complete understanding of your client's business. It is a continuous cycle you can leverage to build the strongest of client relationships.

Pulling It Together:

Leverage the Quadrants to Build the Strongest Relationships

Learn to 2-step.

Giving clients advice on their business is a 2-step process. A word of warning: these may be the 2 most difficult steps to learn.

1. *Understand your client's business as well as they do.*
   Understanding your client's business is the single, most effective differentiator for any professional services firm (I discuss this activity—and how to build your understanding—in great detail in Chapter 3). When you are in the position of giving advice to clients, a thorough understanding of their business and industry is required. In this way you can provide the correct advice to clients, and also discuss—and sometimes defend—the advice you offer.

   Tailored advice for clients means going past the correct answer. It's providing the correct answer in light of the client's situation. Did you consider the current market conditions, the goals and objectives of the management team, the resources needed to implement your recommendation? Even more importantly, if the client takes your recommended course of action, what will the impact be—on them, on the company, on various departments, competitors, and in terms of finances and reputational impact? The list of factors your clients assess on a daily basis is practically infinite.

   Only the most thorough understanding of your client's business will prepare you to have a productive conversation on business issues.

(continued on next page)

(continued from previous page)

An additional—but important—side note: **understand your client as well as you understand their business.** Internal politics, personal motivations, organizational culture, and past experiences with professional services providers are critical considerations for whether a client will invest in or dismiss your advice. Quickly assess your situation in order to deliver your advice in the most appropriate manner possible. Notice, I didn't say target your advice accordingly. Your advice is your advice, but getting buy-in sometimes requires careful attention to your delivery.

2. *Offer pointed, unequivocal advice (and be prepared with 1 or 2 equally thought-out alternatives).*
C-level executives want to know you believe in your own advice. They will judge your conviction and investment in the recommendations you propose. Are you providing truly tailored advice, or simply cookie-cutter recommendations you offer to all your clients? In order to test this, clients will often challenge you and your advice.

C-level executives have a knack for quizzing their service providers on how and why they chose their concluding presentation and often drill professionals on the implications of their advice. Most clients aren't trying to be difficult. Most are kicking the tires (so to speak) and making sure investing in your advice is a sound business decision.

A successful strategy when discussing your recommendations is to use the case study approach. How has similar advice for other clients worked in this situation? What is different given the nuances of this particular project? C-level executives are put at ease when there is a proven track record to back up your recommendations.

CHAPTER 13

Reputation

Clients Will Love You—and Use You—
If They Think Highly of You

YOUR CLIENT'S (OR POTENTIAL CLIENT'S) DIRECT OR INDIRECT experience with you and your organization defines your brand. The collective result of your continuing interactions ultimately defines who you are. Your reputation is the net result of how clients, potential clients, and the business community talk about your brand. Each individual person will put their own spin and nuance on the message and perceived experience with you. Your goal is to maneuver your experience and messaging to have as many people as possible thinking about you in two ways:

1. With uniformity across individuals, clients, potential clients, and markets.
2. Different from and better than others.

Your clients and market at large rely on both direct and indirect experience to develop their opinion about you. These indirect experiences range from people talking about you to your web presence, social media, newsletters, publications, webinars, and similar activities. But, nothing is more powerful than direct experience followed closely by a trusted peer relaying their experience with you.

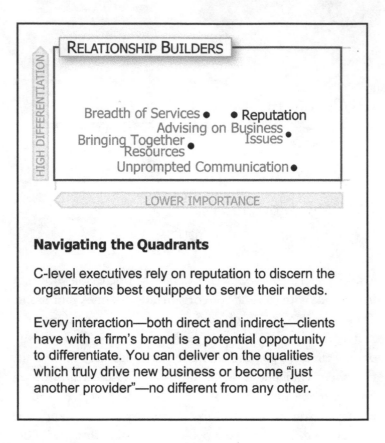

RELATIONSHIP BUILDERS

HIGH DIFFERENTIATION

Breadth of Services ● ● Reputation
Advising on Business ●
Bringing Together ● Issues
Resources ●
Unprompted Communication ●

LOWER IMPORTANCE

Navigating the Quadrants

C-level executives rely on reputation to discern the organizations best equipped to serve their needs.

Every interaction—both direct and indirect—clients have with a firm's brand is a potential opportunity to differentiate. You can deliver on the qualities which truly drive new business or become "just another provider"—no different from any other.

Most of the market will not have had direct experience with you. This means your reputation plays a key role in positioning you to develop a relationship. This also means client referral networks and all the other branding activities are foundational in forming your reputation.

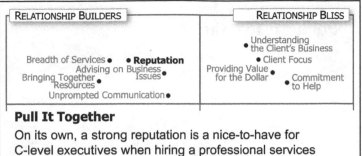

RELATIONSHIP BUILDERS	RELATIONSHIP BLISS
Breadth of Services • • **Reputation** Advising on Business • Bringing Together • Issues • Resources • Unprompted Communication •	• Understanding the Client's Business • Client Focus Providing Value • for the Dollar • Commitment to Help

Pull It Together

On its own, a strong reputation is a nice-to-have for C-level executives when hiring a professional services firm. However, direct or indirect experience (referral or feedback from a peer) will turn reputation from Relationship Builder into Relationship Bliss.

Pulling It Together:

Leverage the Quadrants to Build the Strongest Relationships

Almost everything you do can—and does—impact your reputation. BTI's research shows the following factors with the most impact on relationships and hiring are, in order:

1. Unprompted Referrals about You from Peers
   Fully 57% of C-level executives will hire a new service provider based on a single, unprompted recommendation from a peer. A staggering insight into the power of recommendations—correction: **unprompted** recommendations.

   Unprompted, unaided recommendations mean you earned this recommendation on your own merit. This is like a write-in vote. No one asked about you by name or included you as part of a list—it's the difference between: "How did you like eating at Restaurant ABC?" (Prompted) and "What's your favorite restaurant?" (Unprompted)

2. Quoted in Publications and Media
   Your quotes and quips in respected publications get you noticed by a bevy of top executives. Clients perceive reputable media outlets as being capable of identifying those professionals with the most relevant knowledge on the topic at hand. Clients trust these quotes because you have been vetted by a set of independent editors somewhere in the process.

   Media quotes have marketing value well beyond their initial publication or broadcast. Your quotes are distributed through social and electronic media. You can also easily share the articles featuring your comments with your network. If you can motivate your network to share your quote, you have added peer vetting to your being cited as an authority—boosting the impact on your reputation.

3. Presenting at an Industry Event

   Clients want you to understand their business. (See Chapter 3 for an in-depth discussion.) Your presentation at industry events provides independent evidence you understand more than most because you got yourself on the agenda. Like being quoted in the media, you have been able to convince a third party you have industry knowledge others don't. Potential clients also like the idea of observing you from a safe distance and being able to ask questions without having a conversation. Your clients will be impressed with your ability to stand out.

Well-known Firm Name

Well-known beats unknown if you can't pass muster on the 3 factors above. Clients and potential clients will look for the well-known name when the bigger influencers are absent. This gives hope and power to the smaller firms, upstarts, boutiques, and solos who can make a big impression in the 3 factors above. This also says a well-regarded brand qualifies you for consideration—but you still have other hurdles in your path in the form of the 4 activities in the Relationship Bliss quadrant (Commitment to Help, Client Focus, Understanding the Client's Business, and Providing Value for the Dollar).

In-person Introductory Meeting

These meetings take place when you have networked your way in to meet someone. This meeting will be the beginning of a potential client's direct experience with you. Your ability to get in the door for an in-person meeting means you have passed your prospect's own screening process, which is intense and difficult. But this is only the beginning—BTI's research reveals professionals like yourself will have reached

(continued on next page)

(continued from previous page)

out to a top executive decision maker up to 7 times in order to secure a single meeting. And most of these same executives report routinely declining initial requests for meetings as a filter to test for follow-up activity. Believe it or not—approximately 90% of professionals do not try a second time—which may explain why in-person introductory meetings are less influential in establishing your reputation—unless you are in the 10% who follow up.

Authoring an Article

Authoring an article for the trade press sits at the lower end of reputation building due to the existence of less-than-respectable publishers' "pay-for-play" practices. Executives believe some publishers live on money from authors who pay to publish their articles. These paid articles have a powerful diluting effect on the self-authored articles, as few executives have the time or inclination to separate the credible self-authored articles from the others. However, your self-authored article in a world-class publication with a proven reputation for screening is unquestioned and offers significant value in building reputation.

Social Media—The Wild Cards

Top executives will tell you everyone and anyone, in fact, seems to have a voice on social media. These top decision makers report webinars, online events, blogs and tweets are a sea of comments where they spend little time—unless a peer or trusted source refers something specific with a link to the source. Then you may start making an impact. These top decision makers want to grab hold of new ideas but do not want to curate their own content to find them—they say the payoff is too low.

Social media and online tools can be powerful in building your reputation. The voices with the most impact belong to the professionals who post consistently over time—or develop a killer breakthrough post. But, the most successful posters learn the language which attracts attention and will be shared by others. These successful users of social media develop a theme tied to a specific topic and find different messages to reinforce their theme over and over again.

These wild-card tools can create a reputation for those with discipline and diligence—and create the near equivalent of a direct experience for the very few who can break through the clutter.

Online Events

Online events are much like social media. Top executives are flooded with invitations, and a small number offer insightful content. As a result, online events have little meaningful impact on your reputation—but the few offering deep insights can boost their reputation immediately and keep building reputation.

Advertising

BTI's research consistently shows advertising has little impact on reputation. Top executives rely on direct and indirect experience to drive their thinking about your reputation. Unless you can support multiyear campaigns to hammer home a message, advertising does more to dilute reputation than add.

The Cumulative Effect

Reputation building activities have a powerful, cumulative effect. The more the merrier. Increases in activity generate a proportionately bigger increase in your reputation—enabling you to build a voice, and a reputation.

CHAPTER 14

Unprompted Communication

Information Age Rage

Different from keeping clients informed (see Chapter 8), unprompted communication is a deliberate, systematic effort to maintain ongoing dialogue—both related to and outside of current project work—with clients.

Information and data are the newest currencies in today's business environment. C-level executives are looking to their professional services providers to supply information before being asked for it. Truth be told, professional services firms—in fact, all industries—have heard this message loud and clear. Just look at your email inbox every morning if you have your doubts. There's an ongoing information overload. So why do C-level executives continue to ask for more information from their professional services providers? (They do. In every study I've conducted with this population, at least 54% of clients are looking for their providers to be more proactive in supplying information.)

Let's look at your inbox again. Each morning, how many emails are sitting in there waiting for you? 10? 25? 50? More? How many of those emails do you actually read? If you're anything like me, it's less than 20%. Why so few? Because you know most of those emails are (1) not relevant to you, (2) trying to sell you something you're not interested in, or (3) filled

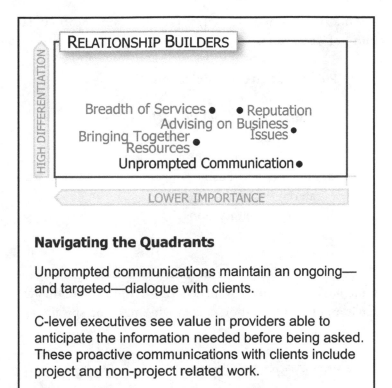

RELATIONSHIP BUILDERS

HIGH DIFFERENTIATION

Breadth of Services ●   ● Reputation
Advising on Business
Bringing Together ●   Issues ●
Resources
Unprompted Communication ●

LOWER IMPORTANCE

Navigating the Quadrants

Unprompted communications maintain an ongoing—
and targeted—dialogue with clients.

C-level executives see value in providers able to
anticipate the information needed before being asked.
These proactive communications with clients include
project and non-project related work.

with far too much information to digest in one sitting—you
might save those to read at a later (usually unrealized) date.

Information is a double-edged sword. C-level executives
want information, but if you send the wrong information—if
it's not relevant or specific to the client—you risk, at best, the
client deleting what you've sent and, at worst, earning the reputation of being not client-focused.

Information and the surrounding communications fall into 1 of 2 categories:

1. Project-related communications
   a. Status updates
   b. Data-sharing, timelines, deliverables
   c. Reporting
2. Non project-related communications
   a. Industry and business updates (newsletters, flash alerts)
   b. Sales communications
   c. Client feedback

Regardless of the type of communication you use, the same holds true: clients want the information before they ask for it and the information you provide must be specific and relevant to them.

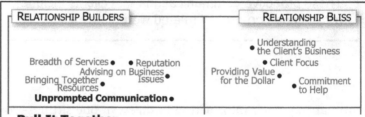

RELATIONSHIP BUILDERS	RELATIONSHIP BLISS
Breadth of Services • • Reputation Advising on Business • Bringing Together • Issues • Resources • **Unprompted Communication** •	• Understanding the Client's Business • Client Focus Providing Value • for the Dollar • • Commitment to Help

Pull It Together

Unprompted communications are only valued by clients when combined with the Relationship Bliss activities. C-level executives are seeking targeted information. They will ask themselves: is this relevant to my business, has this added value for me, is my provider really trying to help me rather than just sell me something?

If a client can answer yes to all 3 of those questions, your unprompted communications will be a positive differentiator for your firm.

Pulling It Together:

Leverage the Quadrants to Build the Strongest Relationships

The power of a well-timed (and well-written) project update

If a client is asking you for information, it's too late. This is especially true as it relates to your project work with a client. The client may think you've dropped the ball or are distracted by something else. Either way, you are left playing defense.

- *Embrace routine updates*
  Monthly, weekly, daily updates—whatever the client's preference. At the onset of a project, confirm how frequently you will send progress updates to the client.
- *Keep your ears tuned*
  Did a client mention an important upcoming management meeting or internal team debrief? Send a comprehensive project update the day before so your client isn't left empty-handed when it comes to answering questions from peers.
- *Immediate notification when something—anything—changes*
  New team members, scope issues, timeline shifts—clients want real-time updates when anything out of the ordinary occurs as it relates to their project. The last question you want your client to ask is, "Why didn't you tell me sooner?" I assure you, there is no good answer.
- *Be upfront with all the information*
  Open lines of communication on all topics make your interactions with clients much smoother. Don't avoid the budget—keep clients proactively updated. If you have initial concerns or foresee potential problems, tell the client as soon as possible so they can start thinking about

(continued on next page)

(continued from previous page)

solutions. Being upfront with clients doesn't make you the harbinger of bad news, it demonstrates you are committed to helping your client be as successful as possible.

The love/hate relationship with blast communications. Dear [insert client name here]...

Few things are as impersonal as today's common blast communications. These are the monthly email newsletters, push alert notifications on emerging news, and generic sales marketing pieces nearly every organization has adopted because there are few ways as effective at reaching a broad base of clients at once. The problem with these communications is most times the information is too broad to be relevant or interesting for every one of your clients. As a tool to keep a dialogue with clients open, it's a fairly poor one. You are unintentionally making clients feel like a part of the herd, instead of part of a valued relationship.

Thinking back to my email inbox for a moment, let me run down the list of criteria I use to decide whether or not to open an email:

- *Did it come from a person or an organization?*
  If a person—and more so, if it's a person I actually know—I am more apt to open the email. I understand we all want to brand our organization, but as professionals, we are in the relationship business. If you really want clients (particularly the busy, decision-making, C-level executives), to read your communications, ditch the impersonal company email and have it come from the relationship contact.
- *Is the subject line (and content) relevant to me?*
  "Monthly Update for 08-2014" isn't going to catch my attention like, "New court ruling is putting BTI at risk. Let's talk." If a subject line mentions topics of interest to me, I am 20 times more likely to open the email

immediately. My first thought is, "I have to read this or else." The topics C-level executives tell me are always of importance to them are:

    a. Emerging regulations or changes in requirements impacting current processes at their organization

    b. Industry trends and breaking news, and the implications for their business operations or objectives

    c. Competitor actions potentially putting their organization at risk

    d. Technological or business process advancements to help make their job easier

- *Can I quickly disseminate the most important information?* Monthly newsletters can sit in someone's inbox for nearly a month before being read. They typically include lots of detailed—but important—information. However, not every item in a newsletter will resonate with each client. As a relationship contact, taking 5 minutes to add a quick intro to your client's newsletter or update can be a strong differentiator. "Hey Michael, check out the fourth article here. It talks about how Competitor X is preparing to launch a new product. Let's set up a time this week to talk through how this impacts our plan." Use any of these 3 sentences to open a value-added dialogue with a client (one likely to spin into some additional work).

    Helping your client get to the most important information quickly sets you apart as being truly committed to helping and increases the value you deliver since the client isn't wading through pages of information trying to find what's important. Without the customization, your email becomes another one they skip.

The client feedback clients want to give

Ask the right questions and clients are happy to talk about the attributes and behaviors defining your superior performance. Most enjoy engaging in a well-designed feedback

(continued on next page)

(continued from previous page)

initiative. Your client wants to provide you with objective information to help you improve. In fact, a client who declines to give you feedback is a client who is no longer invested in your relationship.

Clients enjoy an engaging and thoughtful interview. Clients want to know you are investing in the relationship and are interested enough to keep improving. My company regularly receives thank you notes for conducting an engaging and thoughtful interview. Clients like to engage their minds—and they see this engagement as an extension of your brand.

The most powerful client satisfaction studies target active metrics and track behaviors. These surveys test for behaviors, actions, and inactions. Clients want to comment on the experience and delivery. In fact, 79% of clients state the delivery process is the first criteria in evaluating their advisors. Clients look for wide latitude in their ability to answer. They view your relationship as complex and want the space to mentally unravel the complexity. You can read more about the most powerful client feedback in my upcoming book: *Does This Client Make Me Look Fat?*

CHAPTER 15

Bringing Together Resources
It's Not the Size, but How You Use It

World Law enjoyed a strong relationship with long-term client, Sweet Tech Corp, where billings averaged just over $20 million annually. The senior partner at World Law, Lou, was preparing to retire. As the primary contact with Sweet Tech, he openly shared his retirement plans with Sweet Tech's CEO, Jason. To ease the transition and ensure work was not interrupted, Jason requested a succession and transition plan from World Law.

World Law conducted an exhaustive internal search. Lou, the retiring partner, developed a job specification sheet including technical skills, interpersonal aspects, personal chemistry, and communication style. The firm set up a committee to vet the potential candidates. After a thorough matching of skills and assessment of availability, World Law decided upon Gus as the logical successor to Lou. Lou immediately began incorporating Gus into the relationship—training him on all the processes, bringing him to client meetings, and sharing all the nuances of Sweet Tech one builds from a long-time relationship.

Within the year, Lou retired and Gus took the reins.

6 months later, Jason at Sweet Tech called the managing partner of World Law. Jason was not happy with Gus. Jason acknowledged Gus' technical prowess, but there were numerous chemistry and personality issues eroding the previously strong relationship. Jason expressed respect for Gus and the value World Law brought, but requested a new partner be assigned to manage Sweet Tech's account.

World Law responded quickly. The managing partner went to meet with Sweet Tech to demonstrate concern and understand Jason's every concern and suggestion. World Law initiated a new search.

After several weeks of new partner analysis, the firm reached what it thought was an insightful and telling observation—Gus was in fact the right partner for Jason and Sweet Tech Corp. Every piece of objective evidence—from his location, expertise, past experience, and even understanding of Sweet Tech's operations—supported Gus remaining as partner.

The managing partner, Barbara, took Jason to an outstanding lunch—wonderful food, great view, and the restaurant's well-known power table. Barbara thanked Jason for being such a long-time client and shared the firm's view on how important Sweet Tech is to World Law. Jason was feeling reassured and sensed he would soon be enjoying a relationship with a new partner. At one point, Jason thought he would be invited in to interview potential partners.

But suddenly, Jason felt empty. He was stunned. World Law was recommending Gus remain as the partner in charge of the relationship. Barbara explained how Gus met every criterion and was clearly up to the task. In World Law's opinion, Gus was the best partner for Sweet Tech Corp.

Jason politely shared his disbelief and suggested the firm reassess the assignment. Barbara reiterated she was acting in best interest of Sweet Tech Corp.

Jason thanked Barbara for her time and effort. He went back to his office to develop a transition plan to work with one of the 8 other law firms on his roster.

———————

IN MY 30 YEARS OF CONSULTING, I'VE SEEN SUCCESSFUL PRO-fessional services firms ranging from 1-person shops to global networks of more than 20,000 employees. I've also seen unsuccessful firms at each end of the size spectrum. When it comes to your organization's resources, differentiation and advantage comes from how you use your resources—not how many you have.

Navigating the Quadrants

C-level executives expect you to look across all your available resources—departments, offices, countries, and even networks—in order to provide them with the team best suited to meet their needs.

Clients will assess how well you bring together resources in 2 main ways:

1. C-level executives want to be assured you have taken into account their specific needs—and often their personality—in order to assemble the absolute best resources for their project.
2. Clients are looking for seamless integration of your resources—not disjointed, disparate service delivery. Few things are as frustrating to clients as feeling like you are wrangling fleas when dealing with your professional services provider.

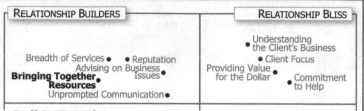

RELATIONSHIP BUILDERS	RELATIONSHIP BLISS
Breadth of Services ● ● Reputation Advising on Business ● **Bringing Together** ● Issues ● **Resources** ● Unprompted Communication ●	● Understanding the Client's Business ● Client Focus Providing Value ● for the Dollar ● ● Commitment to Help

Pull It Together

Resources can be one of the strongest drivers of a superior client relationship. Assembling the right client teams has the potential to demonstrate your ability to deliver on each of the 4 Relationship Bliss activities.

Pulling It Together:

Leverage the Quadrants to Build the Strongest Relationships

Staff projects in a client-focused manner.

Most project staffing and role assignment happens behind the scenes, well before the kick-off meeting with the client. Professionals use experience and their own preferences for whom they want to work with throughout the life of a project. Bringing clients into this critical decision demonstrates you have put thought into searching for the best resources, and proves you are committed to making the relationship— and project—succeed.

- Before project work begins, introduce the entire team to your client
    - > For exceptionally large projects or teams, the major players will suffice
- Explain why each individual has been selected and highlight their unique attributes
    - > Look past the stated needs of your client to introduce a truly custom approach to staffing (are there team members who bring industry—if not exactly technical—insight to a project?)
- Tie the individual's experience to your client's goals or objectives
- In private, ask you client for their thoughts on each selection

(continued on next page)

Be willing to change staffing for good—or even not-so-good—reasons.

Needs change and personalities clash. At some point in your career, a team change is needed. While difficult to deliver the news to your colleagues, the ultimate goal is to make sure the client's needs are met while building a superior relationship. No matter how well suited you believe someone is for the client's work, ultimately the client's opinion matters most.

I have 2 good (and true) stories for how I've seen this last point play out at 2 different providers. We opened the chapter with an example of using resources to help destroy the relationship, and we'll end with its polar opposite—using resources to help build the relationship:

Joe and Steve, 2 engineers from the New York office of a large well-known environmental consulting firm, were sitting down to their annual client meeting with George, the Director of Operations for a Fortune 1000 pharmaceutical company. The 3 men had worked together for more than 15 years and considered each other colleagues and friends. This personal relationship made the news George needed to deliver even more difficult.

"I just received a mandate from the CEO to cut this project's cost by 10%," George began. "You guys don't come cheap," he continued. The engineers began to interrupt, but George stopped them. "Your expertise and experience with the company is invaluable and you are worth every penny—for the most strategic and sensitive components of this project. But I can't justify your costs for the routine drafting and infrastructure audits. Those are tasks any firm can handle at about one-third the cost. So my plan is to keep you on for the overall master planning, but I need to move the more routine work somewhere else."

Joe and Steve thanked George for his candor and asked him to not shift any work for a few days while they went back to the office to "see what we can do for you."

4 days later, the 3 gentlemen met up again, this time joined by 2 other engineers George had not previously met. "George, we'd like to introduce you to Lisa and Dave. Both are junior engineers from our Atlanta office. We've worked with them before and are 100% confident they will be able to handle the drafting and audits for this project. By bringing them onto the team, we'll meet your budget requirements and you also won't have to spend time looking for other providers and onboarding other engineers into the project."

George was ecstatic and the engineering firm successfully prevented a massive loss of revenue while protecting their client from potential poaching by a competitor.

WRAP-UP

Quadrant III
Relationship Builders

THE 5 RELATIONSHIP BUILDER ACTIVITIES CAN BE ENOR-MOUSLY POWERFUL DIFFERENTIATORS FOR YOUR FIRM. C-LEVEL executives seek out relationships with providers able to offer these services. However, delivering these activities without also proving your ability in the Relationship Bliss activities is dangerous. On their own, the Relationship Builder activities can leave clients feeling like you are a one-trick pony well suited for certain matters, but not capable of a sustained long-term relationship where the clients' needs are paramount.

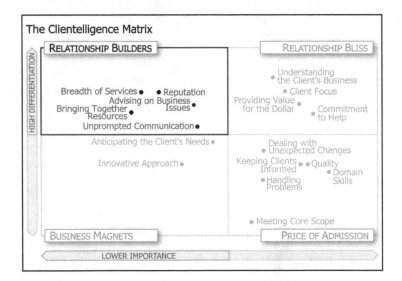

Business Magnets

2 Activities Make C-Level Executives Take Notice

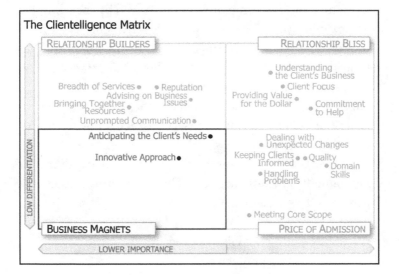

Business Magnets:
The Anomalies

THIS IS WHERE THE ANALYSIS GETS TRICKY. IF YOU WERE TO take the Clientelligence Matrix at face value, you would presume the bottom-right quadrant comprises activities of lower importance and less differentiation to C-level executives. Don't always believe what you see.

When taken as an entire population, the Business Magnet activities did rate lower than other activities in importance and in ability to differentiate a professional services firm. However, my analysis showed an anomaly of sorts when I segmented out the companies I interviewed by spending and complexity of work. The least price-sensitive clients with the most complex needs rated the activities in the Business Magnet quadrant substantially higher in both importance and in the activities' ability to differentiate a professional services firm. So even though fewer clients fit these criteria, they are usually the clients professional services firms are seeking to add to their portfolio.

Hence, the 2 activities in the bottom-left quadrant are aptly named: business magnets. These activities attract new business and new clients:

16. Anticipating the client's need
17. Innovative Approach

A note of caution on the Business Magnet activities: once C-level executives find a professional services firm excelling in these activities, the ongoing relationship is driven by the firm's performance in the Relationship Bliss activities (the upper-right quadrant).

CHAPTER 16

Anticipating the Client's Needs

Developing Your Driver's Vision

Tom and Mark, two brothers who had worked for 26 years to build their company, reached a pinnacle moment. Their now substantial wealth was fully invested in the company. The brothers were reaching a point in their lives where they wanted to ensure the future financial security of their families. After considering a number of options, the brothers were looking at potential acquisitions in order to build the business. Going public seemed to be just the ticket to embark on this new path.

Tom and Mark asked business acquaintances who they might talk with about the process. The brothers received a few referrals, engaged in a few phone conversations, and settled on two advisors who they decided to interview in depth. The two interviews were scheduled for the same day: one in the morning, the other in the afternoon.

Advisor A showed up with a team of four people and their reliable, pitch-winning PowerPoint in hand. Advisor A had done their homework and it showed. The presentation focused on how Advisor A had worked in this industry for years, taken brother-owned companies public, and detailed their understanding of the trusts actually owning the company. Advisor A even managed to work a metaphor on sailing—Mark's passion—into the presentation. The brothers marveled at all the ways the firm was able to touch their experience.

Tom and Mark left the meeting impressed.

Advisor B—just one person—arrived at precisely 1:30. The brothers spent a few minutes on small talk. Ed, the Advisor, asked the brothers to recap their story of how the company got started. Reluctantly, the brothers began—wondering why Ed hadn't done his homework. After 20 minutes, Ed politely interrupted the brothers and asked why they wanted to go public. The brothers reiterated the need for liquidity, their desire to make acquisitions, and ultimately provide for their families.

After listening to the responses, Ed shared an observation about the use of the trusts, like the one used for ownership of Tom and Mark's business. Ed suggested he only sees these kinds of ownership structures when the owners are especially concerned about privacy. Ed asked how the brothers felt about keeping their affairs private. The brothers quickly admitted they harbored a passion for keeping the family affairs private. Ed then produced a list of disclosures the brothers would have to make if they opted to take their company public, none of which the brothers had seen before.

Ed offered two alternatives to going public. Each option would boost the company's liquidity, required virtually no new disclosures, and could be accomplished at a fraction of the cost of going public.

The brothers quickly lost track of the names of Advisor A.

MASSACHUSETTS, MY HOME, REQUIRES ALL PARENTS TO ATTEND a 2-hour driver's education class before their child can take a road test. When my oldest son was preparing to take his test, I mustered all my energy and prepared for an evening of drunk-driving warnings and the secret to making a left-hand turn.

About 20 minutes in, the instructor, Bill Anderson, owner of Anderson's Driving School, started talking about the concept of developing a "driving vision." Bill pointed out how new drivers need to drive between 12,000 and 18,000 miles before they begin to develop their driving vision.

Driving vision is the ability to know where to look and recognize the significance of what is in the road. Most new drivers look 90 feet in front of their vehicle, relying on their central vision to steer the car. Central vision offers detail but is limited to vision directly in front of you.

Experienced drivers look between 90 to 180 feet ahead. They integrate peripheral vision into their driving. While less clear, peripheral vision frequently provides guides and markers for the driver. Any movement, color, or unusual activity is a cue to what lies ahead and provides advance notice of potential hazards, giving the experienced driver time to make adjustments before a potential situation turns dangerous.

Operating in Scan Mode

Much like driving, the only way to anticipate what will come next is by constantly scanning the horizon, interpreting the cues you receive, and preparing for what lies on the road ahead.

In my 35 years of working with C-level executives, I haven't found more than a handful of clients able to fully articulate—or visualize—the entire spectrum of possibilities arising from a project. Clients are keenly focused on their primary objectives, but spend less time considering the Butterfly Effect of what it takes to achieve the outcomes they are seeking. Your role is to help your client understand all the major implications and opportunities that may arise throughout the course of your work with them.

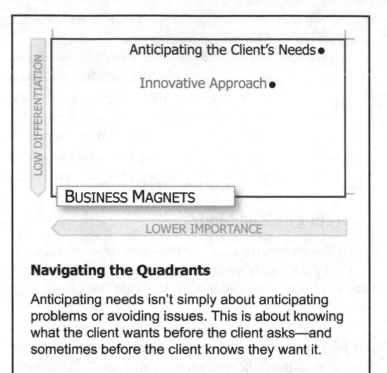

LOW DIFFERENTIATION

Anticipating the Client's Needs●

Innovative Approach●

BUSINESS MAGNETS

LOWER IMPORTANCE

Navigating the Quadrants

Anticipating needs isn't simply about anticipating problems or avoiding issues. This is about knowing what the client wants before the client asks—and sometimes before the client knows they want it.

Successful anticipation of client needs transforms you into a visionary.

The 5 Types of Client Needs

To begin anticipating client needs, you first must understand the types of needs clients face. Clients' needs fall into 5 distinct categories:

1. **Undefined**
   Undefined needs are the hidden opportunities or lurking issues no one is focused on solving—yet. These require a high degree of innovation (see the next chapter) and personal investment to solve. The risk of the unknown, perceived insurmountable obstacles, or the client's inability to articulate a specific need stand in the way of success. Your challenge is to spot these hidden opportunities and provide a solution. The ability to meet an undefined need can differentiate—and elevate—professional services firms, reconfigure entire industries, and shift economics. The more influential examples of meeting undefined client needs include:
   a. The first personal computer
   b. The ability to buy merchandise online
   c. Digital music players

2. **Unmet**
   Unmet needs are those needs where clients have some sense of a defined need but can't articulate or ask for a specific service or scope of work to meet the need. Clients understand there is a potential opportunity or issue, but you still face a client with no predetermined expectation—or solution for moving forward.

3. **Emerging**
   Emerging needs are the needs clients spend most of their energy trying to solve. They are the equivalent of "the next big thing" and risk-averse clients spend a lot of time trying to get ahead of these issues. Meeting emerging needs can be a good base from which to build a

(continued on next page)

(continued from previous page)

relationship, but today's emerging needs are tomorrow's routine needs.

4. **Routine**

Routine needs are, well...routine. They are commonplace but do not gain the client's immediate attention as these needs are easily solved, and quickly and efficiently to boot. Positioning yourself as the provider able to solve a client's routine needs puts you at risk of high price pressure and potential replacement by an automated system.

5. **Fading**

Fading needs are opportunities or issues quickly losing importance. Shifting business objectives, economic factors, or even new management can force past high-priority issues into the realm of unimportance. Continually check on your client's latest thinking and goals to ensure you are meeting forward-looking needs.

The ability to meet undefined and unmet client needs is one of the most powerful client service tools ever discovered. And, the most lucrative areas on the client spectrum of needs. Clients see high value in solving these needs and hold a special place for those professionals who can discern these needs.

Meeting needs—like our driving skills—is developed over time. You begin with a solid foundation of knowledge in order to handle a client's needs. Most professional services firms are adept at meeting routine and even emerging needs. This is code for meeting scope (Chapter 7)—it's a Price of Admission activity and does little to separate you from your competitors. Anticipating needs goes beyond meeting scope. It's the ability to use your experience to develop your peripheral vision and meet the undefined and unmet needs clients have.

Anticipating needs moves you from the client's vendor to a trusted partner.

In the opening to this chapter, both Ed and Advisor A walked into the meeting with the same information. Advisor A simply talked about the depth of their experience and how it applied to the scope Tom and Mark discussed. Advisor A implied success based on past performance—not based on the unique circumstances of this project. Ed, from Advisor B, used his experience to anticipate Tom and Mark's needs and articulated how he would apply the knowledge to their specific situation.

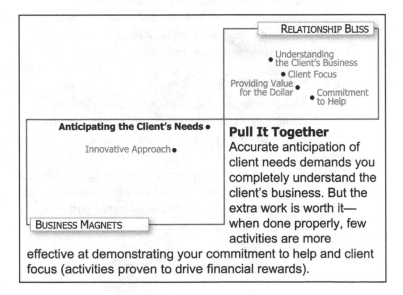

RELATIONSHIP BLISS

• Understanding the Client's Business
• Client Focus
Providing Value for the Dollar •
• Commitment to Help

Anticipating the Client's Needs •

Innovative Approach •

BUSINESS MAGNETS

Pull It Together
Accurate anticipation of client needs demands you completely understand the client's business. But the extra work is worth it— when done properly, few activities are more effective at demonstrating your commitment to help and client focus (activities proven to drive financial rewards).

Pulling It Together:

Leverage the Quadrants to Turn Business Opportunities into Long-lasting Relationships

---

Death by "I did what the client asked."

Anticipating needs is all about staying one step ahead of the client. It demands you constantly think beyond stated scope and scan the horizon for:

- Occasions to make a project sail smoother
- Routes to get the client to their destination faster
- Alternative scenarios to avoid issues likely to cause a bump in the road
- Opportunities to deliver more than what the client has outright requested

The majority of professionals in today's world live by the motto: "I did what the client asked." These professionals, by definition, are not anticipating needs—or adding value.

Anticipating needs doesn't require ESP. A formal approach to tackling a client's issue will get you 90% of the way there (the other 10% is having the guts to trust your instinct).

Step 1: Information Gathering

Engage—don't explain to—clients. Every situation is unique. At a minimum, every client's preferences are unique. The most successful initial meetings with clients focus on gathering the data you need in order to craft a custom solution taking into account as many relevant variables as possible. Asking the right questions at the onset will allow you to provide the best answer. By the end of the information gathering phase, you have broad insight into the following:

- Client's expected outcome
- The driving factors motivating your client
  Motivation is the largest clue for why certain projects are undertaken—it also is the most variable. Clients are motivated by business objectives and personal success goals. Sometimes a lack of understanding of potential options (like Tom and Mark) drives clients down a certain path. Asking the right questions will unveil the subtle—and not so subtle—motivators driving clients.
- Listen for unusual or leading questions or comments such as:
  > So how much work will this be for us?
  > How do CEOs typically react to the results of a project like this?
  > Who else have you discussed this with?
  > Why did X company buy Y company—what did I miss?

All questions and inquiries like these are clues to a concern or issue. Your ability to answer these questions is often the difference between providing a penetrating insight and providing an answer.

- Assess everything the client is saying, including:
  > Specific issues or concerns they raise
  > The client's opinion of the issue's complexity
  > Clues about unstated needs or potential issues like:
    » How the project is being communicated internally
    » Level of involvement from senior management
- Assess everything the client isn't saying, including:
  > How the client acts and behaves—many times you will find a client's action is in direct opposition to what they are saying

(continued on next page)

(continued from previous page)

>> Observe how work flows in the client organization
>> Understand true decision makers vs. points of contact
>> Become an expert in interpreting body language

> Hesitancy to commit
> Silence or lack of response

Step 2: Demonstrate Your Ability to Think Like the Client

Once you have built your understanding of the client and their unique circumstances, you can begin to impart your knowledge—in a client-focused manner. Most C-level executives I've met are not mind readers. In order to demonstrate you are thinking about their needs and concerns, you must tell them. But rather than boasting (or worse, condescending) to the client, educate them in a value-added manner.

- Proactively provide 1 or 2 alternative solutions to the one the client is considering
  > Discuss the benefits and drawbacks of each
  > Allow the client to offer their feedback
- Share insights and lessons learned from prior experiences with this—or similar—clients
- Engage in a scenario-planning session to outline all the possible options and outcomes
- Develop tools to help the client with their needs such as:
  > Checklists
  > Templates
  > Workflow solutions
- Throughout the project, communication with the client will offer additional opportunities to understand their thinking and assess their reactions. I suggest:
  > Discussing your approach and strategy
  > Assessing the impact of key decisions before taking action

> Walking through design sessions well before
  completion
> Proactively discussing the implications of major
  decisions

CHAPTER 17

Innovative Approach

Don't Change Everything, but Change Something

Google, Apple, Amazon, GE—these usual suspects frequently nab top spots on any "Most Innovative Company" hot list. But they are often joined by peers like Nike, Dodge, Michael Kors, Estée Lauder, and Starbucks.

What is my point? Innovation is not technology.

Technology plays a surprisingly small role in innovation delivery. C-level executives (and, in fact, many consumers) believe the overwhelming majority of innovation stems from changes in behavior—not technology.

The most frequent objection I receive when discussing innovation with professional services providers is, "My client isn't looking for me to be innovative; they are looking for me to do my job." However, my research has shown the exact opposite.

Innovation Flies under the Radar

In the B2B professional services world, most innovation occurs in small pockets of activity. A few lone souls in the sea of professionals create new ideas and share them with their clients. Few professional services organizations embrace innovation at a firm-wide level—defaulting, instead, to their tried-and-true practices based on years of experience. The problem

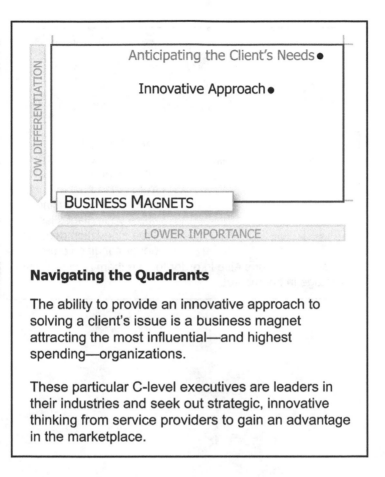

Anticipating the Client's Needs●

Innovative Approach●

LOW DIFFERENTIATION

BUSINESS MAGNETS

LOWER IMPORTANCE

Navigating the Quadrants

The ability to provide an innovative approach to solving a client's issue is a business magnet attracting the most influential—and highest spending—organizations.

These particular C-level executives are leaders in their industries and seek out strategic, innovative thinking from service providers to gain an advantage in the marketplace.

being: a tried-and-true approach is not a competitive advantage, and certainly not a differentiator.

This approach is pervasive throughout the professional services industry—even in seemingly innovative segments such as advertising and healthcare research. My research shows only 26% of C-level executives see professional services providers as innovative.

Even in the midst of some of the most innovative, game-changing technological advances, the vast majority of professional services providers aren't changing their fundamental behavior. New tools; same old solution.

RELATIONSHIP BLISS

• Understanding
the Client's Business

• Client Focus

Providing Value •
for the Dollar
• Commitment
to Help

Anticipating the Client's Needs •

Innovative Approach •

BUSINESS MAGNETS

Pull It Together

Innovation doesn't come from technology. It comes from being able to bring new, creative thinking to solve your client's issues. True innovation demands understanding your client's business like no one else in order to give them a competitive advantage in the market.

Pulling It Together:

Leverage the Quadrants to Turn Business Opportunities into Long-lasting Relationships

Ask yourself, "What business am I in?" and then change your business.

The first rule of innovation is to challenge your assumptions. If Coca-Cola only considered themselves a soda company, the brand would not be the global leader it is today. Instead, the organization focused on being the world's foremost refreshment company, offering soda, water, sports drinks, juice, the list goes on...Coca-Cola granted itself access to a host of beverage products, allowing the company to best serve the current tastes of its customers.

Clients' needs go through a natural lifecycle. A need starts off as a new, unmet issue the client is facing, but will eventually become a routine (even commodity) need, only earning the passing attention of busy C-level executives. Innovation demands solving issues at their most nascent stages— and this requires a constant assessment of what services you actually offer clients.

- An innovative law firm takes a lesson from business consultants to perform workflow assessments to help its clients streamline their own internal operations.
- A Big 4 accounting firm differentiates a commodity service by offering clients an online diagnostic tool to help businesses quickly find answers to financial reporting questions.
- An insurance company helps potential clients better assess their risk by providing an online tool to measure potential costs of large liability-related claims in class action suits.

(continued on next page)

(continued from previous page)

Telling people you are a thought leader usually means you aren't one.

The only way to become a thought leader is to be the first to communicate an issue—and solution—to clients and the marketplace. Thought leadership is a defining aspect of innovation, but few are truly thought leaders; most are thought articulators.

Uncovering and defining issues your clients face requires fast-paced, in-depth research.

- Talk to your clients
  Find out what is next on the horizon for them and their organization.
- Research the market at large
  What trends are most impacting their line of business—particularly ones they aren't sure how to handle?
- Speak with all client-facing individuals at your organization
  Clients share information with us every day, mostly in passing. Tap into the knowledge your employees are gathering. What are clients complaining about? What pressures are they feeling from management?
- Think, think, then think some more
  The information is in front of you, but requires a few brains piecing together new thoughts to paint a clear picture.
  > Encourage everyone—yes, everyone—in your organization to brainstorm the range of issues, underlying drivers, and potential solutions to problems clients and the market face.
  > Put the interns to good use. Data entry and filing can wait. Hire a group of interns to study your data and define the range of key issues, top trends, and unlikely issues arising from your research.

> Read the news when it's supposed to be read. Daily. We all know the saying about yesterday's news...

Stick your neck out.

Client service has been around since the first business opened. Yet finding a true partner—a firm willing to stand by your side and, yes, even argue with the client—is rare, at best. 27% of C-level executives see true innovation stemming from changes in client service delivery.

- Take an unequivocal stand
  You are, I presume, an expert in your field. It's why clients hire you and don't handle the work themselves. So how does bending over to deliver the answer the client hopes to hear—instead of the one they need to hear—help? It doesn't.

  "You think we're fighting, I think we're finally talking!"
  —Rod Tidwell to Jerry Maguire
  (Crowe, Cameron, dir. *Jerry Maguire.*
  Perf. Cuba Gooding, Jr. 1996. Film.)

  Clients enjoy testing you and arguing, but underneath they are looking for you to share your viewpoint and not waver under pressure. Ultimately, clients are hoping your recommendation will bring them to the outcome best for them given their unique situation. C-level executives, in particular, will engage in (sometimes heated) discussions in order to evaluate your solution and make sure it stands up to scrutiny.
  As counterintuitive as it may be, clients only argue with the advisors they hold in the highest esteem. Worry

(continued on next page)

(continued from previous page)

when your client doesn't want to engage with you past a polite discussion.

- Invite the feedback and change
  Client feedback initiatives get a bad reputation because too frequently the study is conducted and nothing changes. Clients are eager to share their opinions on you and your service, but have been burned by professional services providers who seemingly ignore the client's thoughts. True innovation invites your client to have a role in shaping their relationship with you.
    > Ask clients to comment on you—before you start working together
        » Are there team members they would prefer to have as their day-to-day contact?
        » What method and frequency of communication is preferred?
        » What has driven them crazy from you—or other providers—in the past?
        » What's the best thing anyone has ever done for them (from a professional services provider standpoint)?
    > Post-mortems
      After your project has closed, it's time to face the harsh spotlight. Take a bow for the things you did well, and then stiffen your spine to let the client tell you where you fell short. Put systems in place to ensure those missteps don't occur again.
    > Formal client feedback
      Third-party feedback programs capture the most objective responses from clients and can be conducted on a large-scale basis. Your major imperative is to assure the client you heard their feedback and, based on their input, are making changes to improve the relationship.

Relevant value (not value-added).

Tying value (one of the 4 Relationship Bliss activities) and innovation together is the one-two punch of client service. As we discussed in Chapter 4: value is defined by the client—not you. The old adage holds true: clients look for faster, smarter, and cheaper products and services (the joke being, they get to pick 2). Here's how you deliver all 3 to stand out as truly innovative:

1. Faster

   Automation is not just for manufacturing. Automation is equally—if not more—valuable in professional services where streamlining typically frees up valuable time of limited human resources. Automating work processes reduces the amount of time and effort required to complete a project. The number of opportunities to automate is seemingly endless. Expense reporting, data entry, presentation development, and accounting are just the tip of the automation iceberg. Leveraging IT and redistribution of responsibilities gives professional services firms the ability to deliver better service faster, and, often, cheaper.

   Automation 101: Document every work step and activity required to complete a task. Include the order in which the steps are performed and the resources used for each activity. Remove duplicate and nonproductive steps. Identify routine steps—filling out forms, gaining approval, entering information into a database—eligible for automation.

2. Smarter

   Teaching your client something new will immediately make you a thought leader in their eyes. Of course, it needs to be related to their goals.

(continued on next page)

(continued from previous page)

Education creates an impenetrable bond with clients. Education is personal, shows your understanding of their business, and demonstrates your commitment to helping them succeed.

3. Cheaper

Fixed-price billing was one of the key drivers behind consulting behemoth Accenture's initial growth. The fixed-price approach served as an innovative game-changer in a field where clients report it's more difficult to see substantial differences among providers.

The good—make that, great—news for providers: 31% of professionals enjoy *higher* profits after they switch to alternative billing structures. Clients are drawn to alternative pricing because these arrangements typically offer predictability in budget and invite shared risk by the client and their provider. In some cases, the provider only gets paid if they deliver the results the client expects.

Quadrant IV
Business Magnets

THE 2 BUSINESS MAGNET ACTIVITIES ARE YOUR MOST POWER-
FUL TOOLS FOR GENERATING NEW BUSINESS—BOTH WITH
existing and new clients. The ability to deliver on these 2 activities while filtering in behaviors from the Relationship Bliss
quadrant will create a system for your firm to develop new
work and keep clients from thinking about taking their business anywhere else.

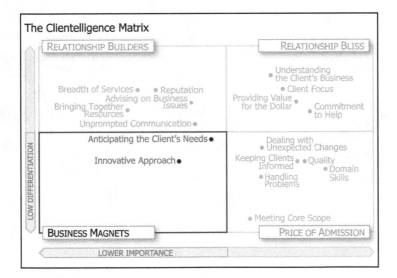

Clientelligence:

The Easiest—and Hardest—
Things to Change

EACH OF THE 17 ACTIVITIES WITHIN CLIENTELLIGENCE IS A behavior-based approach to client relationships. These are activities you can learn—and improve upon—over time. The only investment absolutely required is time—and the fortitude and desire to modify your own behavior.

The Best Way to Start Is to Start

The Relationship Bliss activities are most strongly correlated to financial performance (see Appendix 2). If I'm deciding where to start focusing my efforts to improve client relationships, I'm going to look there. If you can deliver on the 4 most strategic activities, you will deliver on the other 13 in a meaningful way since all the activities are interrelated on some level.

Change is a funny thing. When we make up our mind to change, we get excited and try to change everything at once. Stop. This will never work. You are too busy. Ultimately, you end up abandoning your entire plan. Instead, focus on achieving smaller, sustainable wins.

Is there an activity you are drawn to? Does one of the top 4 activities resonate a little louder than the others? Start there. The first activity, no matter which one you choose, will be the hardest because it's the first. In tandem, pick an already strong client relationship to use as you develop your skills. When improving client service, it's difficult for things to go so wrong as to threaten an existing relationship. The worst outcome is the client didn't see your new approach as value-added (a sign to talk to the client to better understand what it is they are hoping to achieve). However, the added confidence and trust with an established client relationship will allow you to develop and master these skills.

Once you master the first skill, you will find it easier and quicker to introduce the other skills into your client service portfolio.

A Thousand Days in 11-minute Increments

Mastery of a skill requires practicing for a thousand days, not practicing a thousand ways. Once you start practicing superior service skills, don't stop for a long, long time. The goal is to make superior service a muscle memory—a natural, unconscious part of your daily life with clients.

How can a busy professional possibly dedicate 1,000 days to developing a skill? Start with 11 minutes a day or, if you prefer, one hour a week. The key is to pick a pattern you like and stick to it.

Say you want to start by improving your understanding of your client's business—a strong starting point as this activity will differentiate you most in the eyes of your client. Let's set up your first month of tasks:

Week	Tasks

Week 1
 	
Set up continual information flow regarding your client's business
	Establish comprehensive alerts and news tracking for your client's organization. Include:
	Client organization name
	• Individual brand, trade, and subsidiary names
	• Top executives, by name
	• Stock prices
	• Job listings
	• Competitor organizations
	• Company, subsidiaries, etc.
	  > Executives
	  > Stock prices
	  > Job listings

Week	Tasks
Week 2 Identify forward-looking goals for your client's business	• Listen in on an earnings call (for publicly held clients) • Request—and read—your client's most recent business and strategic plan • Download and read your client's annual report

Week	Tasks
Week 3 Assess competitor strategic plans to identify potential threats or missed opportunities for your clients	Same steps as Week 2—but for your client's major competitors

Week	Tasks
Week 4 Build an objective, but informed, outside opinion on your client's business and strategy	• Read what stock analysts are predicting for your client's company—and their competitors • Subscribe to related industry or trade journals and news sites to track emerging issues impacting your client's business

Week	Tasks
Bonus: Week 5 Share your knowledge with your client in a value-added manner	Begin to compile the information you have learned to answer one of the following questions for your client: • What risk is your client not considering? • What are the unexpected opportunities in the market? • How can your client outmaneuver the competition? Posing one of these often unasked questions and providing a potential answer to your client will open a discussion into your client's thinking and offer potential new ways for you to help solve some of their most pressing issues.

A consistent and systematic approach to developing superior client service skills will give you unparalleled access to your clients' most complex—and premium-rate—work, all while your competitors are left wondering how you are always one (or five) steps ahead.

Epilogue:

Anticipating YOUR Needs:
What Comes Next?

You own your behaviors. Your client owns their perceptions of your behaviors. Clients will see your actions through
their own filter. They measure your performance according to
their needs, past experiences, expectations, and interactions
with other professional services providers. Your only chance
to honestly assess your client relationships and understand
how you are really performing on the 17 activities is to ask for
feedback.

As a researcher, it would be next-to-impossible for me not
to include a discussion on the importance of measuring and
assessing your performance in a meaningful and objective
manner. However, I will do my best to contain my enthusiasm
and, instead, focus on the big picture.

The 17 activities within Clientelligence are proven drivers
to superior client relationships. In essence, they are how clients define client service excellence and what they expect out
of the providers with whom they have the best relationships.
As my research has shown, the best-in-class performances in
these activities drive positive financial performance. When
money is potentially on the line, I feel it necessary to do more
than assume we know our clients' thoughts. A few points to
consider:

Step 1: Simple, direct measurement

I have analyzed more than 100,000 data points from 26 independent and 300 client-sponsored studies. These studies all show the most effective way to measure overall performance is to ask clients for quantitative ratings. A 1 to 10 scale works best. This gives clients the room to articulate nuanced performance variations without overly limiting the client's response.

The one question to measure and drive superior relationships and gauge how your clients are (or are not) investing in the relationship is:

On a scale of 1 to 10, with 10 being the absolute best, how well does your professional services provider perform in each of the following activities:

    a. Client focus
    b. Commitment to help
    c. And so on…

You can look at how clients score you in each activity to determine where your organization has institutional strength and where potential weaknesses are lurking. Knowing this information will help you target resources to leverage strengths and eliminate weaknesses quickly.

- **9 or higher**
  You are strongly positioned and performing at top levels in the activity being rated. It is important to maintain a top performance by ongoing commitment to current initiatives supporting the activity. Conduct routine assessments to ensure you continually exceed client expectations.
- **Between 8 and 9**
  You are only mildly differentiated in your performance.

Your performance is not threatening the client relationship, but in order to reap the full financial benefits of the 17 activities, a stronger performance is needed.

- **Between 7 and 8**
  You're skating on thin ice. When conducting research for my own clients, if I see 7s in their rankings, I recommend immediate intervention. A 7 is the equivalent of a C grade—no one is too proud of those. 7s are the weak spots in your relationship, points of frustration for your clients limiting your growth potential and possibly threatening the sustainability of a long-term relationship. Special attention is needed here.
- **6 and below**
  If a client is scoring you a 6 (or lower), you have passed the tipping point. These areas are the thorns in the side of your client. Without immediate intervention and correction, the relationship is at risk. The fact is, in the client's eyes, you are now simply a vendor and the client is actively looking to invest—emotionally and financially—in a different provider.

Step 2: Performance comparison

I have seen the rankings above and their implications proven time and time again. The one exception: when clients rate a competitor higher in any of the activities—no matter the score they assign to you—the relationship is at risk.

In the past 8 years, BTI added a new component to our client studies. As part of each client feedback program we conducted for our clients, we asked their clients to provide ratings on each of the 17 activities for their professional services provider (BTI's client) and another direct competitor the client used. Adding a competitor's score turns a standard definition snapshot into a high-resolution image. You have both an absolute and relative assessment of your performance.

This additional information allows us to compare performance against competitors our clients were facing on a daily basis to assess if the relationship was at risk—and who, by name, was threatening the relationship. Let's face it: it doesn't matter how well we're performing if someone else serving our client is doing it better.

Interestingly, when we added this component to our analysis, this comparative rating was usually the strongest motivator to inciting professionals to change their behaviors. Nothing like a friendly (or not-so-friendly) rivalry to get adrenaline flowing in professionals.

I said I would keep this discussion high level, and I will stick to my word. But let me close by saying, without feedback we are operating on luck—and I'm not willing to bet my salary on presumption.

Of course, if you are interested in learning about the ins and outs of establishing and implementing your own client feedback program, you can learn more by contacting us at www.bticonsulting.com.

Clientelligence Quick Start Guide

Remembering 17 different activities can be a bit overwhelming, particularly when you are beginning to reshape your approach to client relationships. Below is your Quick Start Guide for navigating the quadrants and each of the activities:

Quadrant I: Relationship Bliss

The 4 most influential activities correlated to higher profits and growth. These are the attributes around which you can truly differentiate your firm in the eyes of clients.

1. **Commitment to Help**
   C-level executives make a highly subjective judgment about a professional's investment in the relationship. Clients are drawn to those professional services providers demonstrating a level of commitment matching—or exceeding—the client's own commitment.
   Commitment to help is the most influential activity in a client relationship.
2. **Client Focus**
   Client focus is about meeting the client's targeted outcome, not just providing the most indisputable advice. Client-targeted goals can—and usually do—demand an approach vastly different from the best possible solution. Factors to take into account include: budget, management goals, risk tolerance, and shareholder influence.

3. **Understanding the Client's Business**
   The ability to provide your service in the context of the client's business will most differentiate you in the eyes of C-level executives. Industry dynamics, current events, emerging regulations, competitor news, and political landscape are the basis for providing targeted advice to help clients meet their ultimate objectives.
4. **Providing Value for the Dollar**
   Value is about delivering more than what the client expects. True value is not about lowering rates, it's about delivering what clients value most: saving clients time, providing better outcomes than expected, increasing revenue streams, and bringing them to market faster.

Quadrant II: Price of Admission

These are the minimum requirements a professional services provider needs in order to enter into a relationship with a C-level executive. These attributes will earn you consideration for hire, but do not differentiate you or your firm enough to ultimately win the work.

5. **Domain Skills**
   This is the experience and expertise demonstrating a professional services provider has the ability to handle a client's work. Domain skills are the most important of the 17 activities, but a poor differentiator for firms as most providers bring the level of expertise needed to fulfill the scope of work.
6. **Quality**
   Consistency in final work products, attention to detail, clear and efficient processes, and limited errors act as indicators of quality. Quality is an important attribute most clients only notice when it's lacking.

7. **Meeting Core Scope**

   A project's scope sets the expectations and boundaries of the work to be provided—and C-level executives presume you will deliver the agreed upon work. This biggest missteps occur when scope changes and professionals do not accurately communicate these changes to clients on a timely basis.

8. **Keeping the Client Informed**

   C-level executives want virtual real-time knowledge of progress, changes, challenges, and outcomes resulting from your work. An absence of communication is viewed as a signal of a poor result or a professional's lack of interest in the project.

9. **Dealing with Unexpected Changes**

   Unplanned changes are a part of business and C-level executives seek professional services providers able to roll with the waves. The ability to nimbly alter course, provide new solutions, and limit the number of issues is a skill clients demand of their professional services firms.

10. **Handling Problems**

    Unlike unexpected changes, problems are always bad. At a minimum, C-level executives will look to their professional services providers to accept responsibility (whether or not the provider is at fault) and provide quick solutions to the issues at hand.

Quadrant III: Relationship Builders

C-level executives see the Relationship Builder activities as nice to have in their professional services providers. On their own, they have minimal lasting impact, but combined with activities in the Relationship Bliss quadrant, these 5 activities help sustain and grow long-term client relationships.

11. **Breadth of Services**
    The ability to bring a wide breadth of services to clients is viewed as an asset facilitating their own internal management. Professional services providers able to deliver multiple services leverage knowledge transfer to adopt client-focused approaches and better address client needs.

12. **Advising on Business Issues**
    C-level executives want informed opinions and unwavering recommendations. The ability to provide business advice separates clinical analysis from high-value, strategic counsel.

13. **Reputation**
    C-level executives rely on reputation to discern the organizations best equipped to serve their needs. As a core component of branding, a strong reputation puts you more frequently in the sightlines of decision makers.

14. **Unprompted Communication**
    Different than keeping clients informed, unprompted communication is a deliberate, systematic effort to maintain ongoing dialogue—both related to and outside of current project work—with clients. These communications only build client relationships when they are client-specific, relevant, and personal to C-level executives—otherwise you are lost in the mass of information being sent to clients on a daily basis.

15. **Bringing Together Resources**
    Bringing together resources isn't about how many professionals you have, but how you leverage your resources to meet your client's needs. C-level executives want to be assured you have taken into account their specific needs—and many times personality—in order to assemble the absolute best resources for

their project. Clients are looking for seamless integration of your resources, not disjointed, disparate service delivery.

Quadrant IV: Business Magnets

The 2 activities proven to develop business with new and existing clients—and in particular, large-spending clients with complex needs.

16. **Anticipating the Client's Needs**
    Jump to a C-level executive's top-of-mind list by knowing and delivering what they want before they ask. Avoiding risks, navigating the market from a forward-looking mindset, and being the first to deliver emerging information is considered a business advantage—and worthy investment—to clients.

17. **Innovative Approach**
    Innovation goes well beyond leveraging technology. Clients are drawn to professional services providers able to bring unique, new, or creative thinking to deliver better outcomes and strategic advantages for their business.

Appendix 1:

Identifying and Quantifying the 17 Activities

In 1989, BTI launched its first independent study with buyers of professional services. Over the course of 25 years, 14,000 individuals participated in telephone interviews lasting between 6 and 54 minutes. The goal of these interviews was to uncover the drivers and critical influences in the C-level executive's buying decisions, evaluation, and expectations of professional services providers.

The following open-ended question was asked of all respondents:

On a scale of 1 to 10, with 10 being extraordinarily difficult, how easy is it for you to find a professional services provider delivering the following activities?

- Advising on Business Issues
- Anticipating the Client's Needs
- Breadth of Services
- Bringing Together Resources
- Client Focus
- Commitment to Help
- Dealing with Unexpected Changes
- Domain Skills
- Handling Problems
- Innovative Approach
- Keeping the Client Informed
- Meeting Core Scope
- Providing Value for the Dollar
- Quality
- Reputation
- Understanding the Client's Business
- Unprompted Communication

More than 6,000 responses to these quantitative questions were used to plot each activity's placement in the final chart.

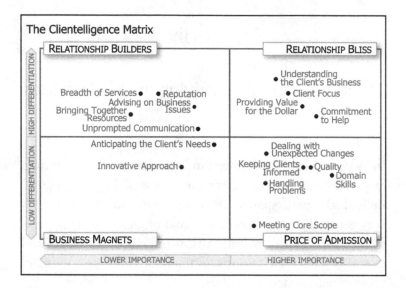

The Clientelligence Matrix

RELATIONSHIP BUILDERS | RELATIONSHIP BLISS

HIGH DIFFERENTIATION

Breadth of Services •   • Reputation
Advising on Business •
Bringing Together •   Issues •
Resources •
Unprompted Communication •

Understanding
• the Client's Business
• Client Focus
Providing Value •
for the Dollar •   • Commitment
to Help

LOW DIFFERENTIATION

Anticipating the Client's Needs •

Innovative Approach •

Dealing with
• Unexpected Changes
Keeping Clients • • Quality
Informed   • Domain
• Handling   Skills
Problems

• Meeting Core Scope

BUSINESS MAGNETS | PRICE OF ADMISSION

LOWER IMPORTANCE | HIGHER IMPORTANCE

Appendix 2:

Statistically Tying Clientelligence to Superior Financial Performance

Once the 17 activities were defined and quantified in terms of importance and differentiation, we set out to correlate a professional services firm's performance in these activities to financial benefits.

Methodology

BTI calculated the Pearson product moment correlation coefficient, r, to test the strength and direction of the linear relationship between each of the 17 activities and a professional services firm's growth.

To do this, BTI interviewed buyers of professional services and asked them to identify, by name, the firms they see as performing at best-in-class levels in each of the 17 activities. BTI's team performed in-depth secondary research to gather financial data for the institutions named. This allowed the team to perform a regression analysis to estimate the relationships among financial variables and client service performance.

Result

The strongest correlation was uncovered in the activities in the top-right quadrant (Relationship Bliss), as documented in the chart below:

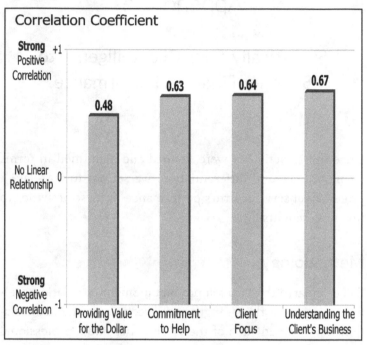

For those of us a little farther removed from *Statistics 101* than BTI's analytical team of MBA graduates, the above chart can be translated as:

> A strong positive linear correlation, when *r* (the correlation coefficient) is close to +1, exists for each of these activities on an individual basis. Meaning, as your performance in an activity increases, your growth will also increase.

Resources

For weekly explorations of ways to continually improve your Clientelligence, subscribe to Michael's blog at www.themadclientist.com.

Visit www.bticonsulting.com to download the most up-to-date white papers on superior client service, and to order Michael's latest books:

The Mad Clientist's ABCs of Client Service

And coming soon:
Does This Client Make Me Look Fat?
The Mad Clientist's B is for Business Development

Want to Know More about Your Clientelligence?

For more information on BTI's research or Michael Rynowecer's seminars, books, and workshops, please contact:

The BTI Consulting Group
396 Washington Street, Suite 314
Wellesley, MA 02481
United States
Telephone: +1 617 439 0333
Fax: +1 617 439 9174

You can also email Michael directly:
mrynowecer@bticonsulting.com

On the web: www.bticonsulting.com and www.themadclientist.com

About the Author

Michael, as President and Founder of The BTI Consulting Group, looks at every angle of the professional services relationship starting with the client perspective. This fascination has driven him to direct, conduct and analyze more than 14,000 one-on-one interviews with C-level executives to define their expectations, needs, priorities, preferences, hiring decisions and opinions of the professionals with whom they work.

Michael draws on this research and his 35 years of experience to provide high-impact client feedback, brand preference and perception, business development counsel and strategic consulting to organizations who want to improve performance and drive growth.

Michael has authored more than 40 publications on all aspects of client relationships, client service, client feedback, client satisfaction, business development and business strategy. Michael blogs at TheMadClientist.com.

CPSIA information can be obtained
at www.ICGtesting.com
Printed in the USA
BVHW032321230322
632214BV00006B/526/J